The Great
The Grand
AND THE
Also-Ran

Rabbits & Champions on the Pro Golf Tour

The Great The Grand
AND THE
Also-Ran

Rabbits & Champions
on the Pro Golf Tour

DAN GLEASON

Random House
New York

Library of Congress Cataloging in Publication Data

Gleason, Dan.
The great, the grand, and the also ran.

1. Golf—Tournaments—History. I. Title.
GV970.G55   796.352'64   75–35657
ISBN 0–394–49054–1

The author thanks Arc Music Corp. for permission to reprint lyrics from the song "The Promised Land" by Chuck Berry (pages19–20). Copyright © 1964 by Arc Music Corp. Used by permission of the publisher; All rights reserved.

Manufactured in the United States of America
9 8 7 6 5 4 3 2
First Edition

*This book and
the efforts that
went into writing it
are dedicated to the
two people who have
helped me most:*
Doc Gleason
and
William Price Fox

Without implying comparison, I am reminded of Melville's *Moby Dick*. What is *Moby Dick* about? Is it a book about whaling in the nineteenth century? Indeed it is. It probably contains more information on the subject than any learned treatise written before or since. Nevertheless, any schoolboy knows that *Moby Dick* is not *really* about whaling. It is about man's hopes, his struggles, his triumphs, and his failures. It is about trying to attain the unattainable—and sometimes making it. And, on its own terms, that is also what this book is about.

—Lawrence S. Ritter
The Glory of Their Times

Contents

Part 1

THE OPENING DRIVE

1

Humble Beginnings: America on $60 a Day

The practicalities of life were discussed in the classified section of the LA *Times*—

> *Marriages performed—*
> *anytime, anyplace, any faith*
> *Contact Mr. Diggers*
>
> *Free pregnancy tests*
>
> *Blood donors needed*
> *Top money*
>
> *Toilet attendant, night shift*
> *Very nice place*
>
> *Divorces—*
> *anytime, anyplace, any faith,*
> *Contact Mr. Diggers*

—while the sports section of that December 31 took you far away from those hard realities and told you, among other things, that a hundred and fifty professional golfers would be playing for more money in one four-day week than all those blood donors—and even the very pragmatic Mr. Diggers—could hustle in three years.

It was the beginning of a new season.

A new season that might not last a month for Rod Curl, a touring pro who had never finished in the top hundred money winners his first four seasons and had barely made ends meet. Now he was what they call *up against it.* He had no backers, no savings accounts, no credit cards, just three weeks' expense money, a wife and two kids, and a 1966 Mercury which was in need of some front-end work. Going into his fifth season on the tour, aside from being five foot five and three-quarters Wintun Indian, Curl was so uncelebrated as a professional athlete that he'd have a hard time cashing a ten-dollar check, even in a tournament town.

He cleaned frost off the windows of the Merc and packed the trunk in his analytical way, trying to get the maximum amount of gear into the minimum amount of space, making sure there was room for all the clubs and balls and baby clothes and radios and maps and suitcases and shoes and coolers and even a 99-cent plug-in device for heating coffee, tea and soup in motel rooms. It was almost six hundred miles from the northern California town of Redding, where they lived, to Los Angeles, where the first tournament of the season would be held, the first of more than forty such tournaments that would be spread out through the year—a long season which would finally end in Florida in early December at the Magic Kingdom of Walt Disney World.

Curl was a hometown Redding boy who, because he was an Indian, drew a few lines in the golf magazines when he got his tour card. Since then, he hadn't done much. Historically, the Wintu Indians were farmers and hunters, and at one time had owned most of the state of California. The Wintus weren't reservation Indians, and Curl had grown up in the white man's ways, having earned their respect by being good at their games—mainly pool and baseball and football as a kid. He made his spending money as a high school kid by playing 9-ball on the front table of a place ironically called the Covered Wagon.

They had big card games in the Covered Wagon, and Curl used to watch to see who won, how and why.

It was fun growing up in Redding, being the star and winning most of the time at most of the things he did. But then high school ended and the baseball career he'd dreamed of never came. For a time he thought of being a professional pool player. It lasted about a month. Bakersfield, Sacramento, San Francisco. It was too hard, and even though he wasn't hustling, there was still the fear of getting his head beat in.

He got married and went to work on construction at the age of eighteen, when $125 a week seemed like big money. But digging ditches and puddling cement got old fast. He wanted to be a pro—a pro something, a pro anything.

He took up bowling, but he analyzed how much it would cost to rent all the shoes and bowl all the lines it would take to get good enough to be a pro. He forgot about bowling.

And then, in 1963, when Curl was nineteen, his father-in-law asked him to go out and play a round of golf. Curl had seen Arnold Palmer on TV and he decided to take a crack. In two months he was a six-handicapper, in six months he was a two-handicapper. In three years he qualified for the U.S. Open as an amateur and played a round with Palmer.

The good thing about golf was that he could practice for nothing once he had the equipment. All he needed were practice balls, clubs and a field to hit them in. He practiced whenever and wherever, dug sand traps in his yard, worked nights to play days, and bought and studied a Ben Hogan instruction book, which, although he hadn't been much of a student in high school, he found fascinating.

In 1968, after going through sectional qualifying, he borrowed $1,500 from his half-sister Esther and went to Palm Beach Gardens, Florida, to try to qualify for his tour card. He had to play eight rounds against some of the top players in the world. Every day he seemed to be out of contention, but he hung in and got his card by one shot, making him one of the fifteen players that year who were eligible to go out onto the tour and, possibly, starve.

Esther and some hometown friends did what they could to back him the first four seasons while Curl existed in obscurity, trying to learn what most other tour pros already knew about the game. After the past season and $18,000 in winnings, he thought he'd find a backer, but he didn't.

He would be hard-pressed, what with caddie fees and motels and meals and gas and oil and God knows, to get by on $400 a week. After two of the four rounds in each tournament, the field was cut to the low seventy places including ties. A player who missed a cut wouldn't get to finish the tournament or make a check. If Curl missed three or four cuts in a row, he'd be history.

Curl was a "rabbit," the jargon for a player who hadn't finished in the top sixty money winners the previous season and had to qualify on Mondays just to get into the tournaments. Making a cut got a rabbit into the next tournament. But if he missed the cut, he'd be back out there again on Monday trying to qualify against sometimes as many as a hundred rabbits for six or seven spots open in a tournament.

Palmer or Nicklaus or any of the top sixty players from the season past could miss a cut and still be exempt from Monday qualifying. They could pick their spots. They got offers for exhibitions, endorsements.

The rabbits hop from town to town nibbling on the lettuce that the top players leave them. A top sixty player can think about winning, while the rabbit has to think about making cuts. The kind of shot you hit with $300,000 in your pocket with the pin tucked left near the big sand bunkers is a screaming hook that will give you the birdie putt. But the kind of shot you hit with $1,423, a wife and two kids, and a '66 Mercury with a bad front end is a safe fade to the fat of the green to assure two putts and the cut.

The difference between sixtieth and sixty-first place is like the difference between being born on the north bank and the south bank of the Rio Grande.

If Curl misses qualifying, he'll be too far from home to go there. He wouldn't want to stay in a town if he isn't in the tournament. So he'll go on to the next town. The members at the courses where the qualifying will be the next Monday don't want a lot of rabbits hanging around and playing their courses all week. So the rabbits might end up at some scroungy driving range all week, while their confidence and their desire and their patience leave them. Little things begin to bother them. After a few years and a lot of disappointments, they're beat down like tank-town fighters.

And after week after week and year after year, the Ramada Inns start looking just like the Holiday Inns, Charlotte in '67 looks just like Fort Worth in '69, and everything tastes like chicken.

And just when they start getting things straight, one season ends, another begins, they jack the prize money up a few thousand more, they run Jack Nicklaus's and Johnny Miller's totals back to $000,000.00, rookies come out with high hopes, and Arnold Palmer gets one year older.

And the rabbits and the $100,000 players all start even on the first tee on the first day. The equality usually ends at the first ball-washer.

Nicklaus and Palmer play in one tournament a week when they play. But Curl will be playing in three tournaments within each tournament—one on Monday to try to qualify, one on Thursday and Friday to try to make the cut, and one on Saturday and Sunday to try to make a big enough check to do it all over again.

This week it was the Glen Campbell LA Open. Curl wondered how long the Merc would last as he finished packing it full. And he wondered how long he would last. His foundation was a little more sound than the Merc's. When he first came out on the tour he averaged only about 230 yards off the tee, which made him shorter than most of the other pros. But he discovered a secret. He'd tried a lot of things—getting his hips and legs into the swing, increasing his swing arc—and some of them worked. Then by accident, he found a way to hit the ball farther than he'd ever hit it in his life.

At one tournament the season before, he teed a ball up on a scorer's pencil to try to get over some trees and cut a dogleg. The ball went straight, it didn't fade over the trees. And it went farther than he'd ever hit a ball before. In his analytical way, he began to think about what made the ball go farther. He studied things like trajectory and leverage and began to experiment. He had been using a Hogan ball, but he found out that a Titleist ball would go higher, stay airborne longer. He worked on changing his set-up and started teeing the ball twice as high as he had before. And now, in spite of his size he was one of the

longest hitters on the tour. Which would make the
game a lot easier.

And now, if he could last the first four weeks, he
could put some of his theories to work. He wished he
knew somebody with enough pull to get him sponsor
exemptions. Sponsors of the tournaments are allowed
to pick eight players who will be exempt for their
tournament. They're usually looking for players from
the local area who might be popular, or some player
with some notoriety who's missed the top sixty but
might be a good gate draw. But the exemptions are
political too. A player with some connections might
be able to get into a tournament via sponsor exemption over a player who, on all other factors, is more
qualified.

But as that season opened, Curl was among the
unconnected.

He'd be living week by week. If he made a cut and
his friends missed it, he wouldn't see them again until the next week. If his friends missed qualifying the
next Monday, they might leave and he would miss
them again. Sometimes he might not see his friends
for months at a time.

There are a lot of rabbits out there on the road
every season. It used to be that the tournament committees had a hard time fielding a tournament. But
now, with the big money that has come to golf, a lot
of athletes have come out thinking pie-in-the-sky. Today, even to finish in the top sixty, a player has to beat
a lot of scrambling, gambling, hungry rabbits like
Rod Curl.

Who filled his car with gas at a station on the outskirts of Redding, opened the hood and unscrewed the
top of the breather, took it off and turned it upside
down, exposing the air cleaner. It was a trick he'd
learned from his brother Gene, who used to race a few

stock cars. It would help stretch his fuel two or three miles a gallon.

Their daughter Suzanne, now three years old, was riding in the back playing with her dolls. Rodney, Jr., was six months old, and he slept quietly in the front in his mother Bonnie's arms while she checked a road map of California.

They stopped to eat at a chili parlor with a lot of teenage chewing gum on the bottoms of the tables. Arnold Palmer would be due in town in his private jet in a few days, and his fan club would be there to meet him at the airport. The Curl family rode into LA behind a street sweeper that night and checked in at an economy motel. They bought 7-Up's and potato chips and cookies, and tea and soup to heat with the plug-in heater. They welcomed in the New Year watching Clark Gable and Spencer Tracy in a movie called *Boom Town.*

And early the next morning, Curl drove through the empty streets and the past night's crepe paper toward LA Country Club to try to qualify. It was Monday, not a day of celebration on the pro golf tour. On the practice tee, Curl talked to Mac McLendon, a pro who'd been losing his game and his confidence the past few seasons. Although he wasn't yet thirty, he looked older, partly because of Mondays and disappointments.

Like the disappointment the season before. McLendon was in sixtieth place going into the last tournament of the season. He asked for a sponsor exemption at the Walt Disney World Golf Classic, and the committee had said yes. But when he got to the tournament, he found out they had given it to a player who'd earned only $5,300 for the season. When he went down to qualify, his hand was bothering him and he didn't get into the tournament. By Thursday the hand had healed, but he wasn't in the tournament. He had to sit on the sidelines and watch Ken Still win $2,550 and move into sixtieth place, forcing Mac McLendon out and putting him back out there on Mondays.

McLendon was harboring serious thoughts about leaving the tour.

They held the qualifying at LA Country Club and it took 72 to play off for one of the six spots open in the LA Open. Curl's 77 didn't get close, and he and his family headed for Santee and the Carlton Oaks, where they would get a break on a motel. Steve Oppermann, a former tour player, owned a motel down around there called the Bayside. He was giving Curl a special rate that turned out to be practically free.

Once they checked in, the room looked like all the other rooms—putters and irons and golf balls scattered all around, yardage cards and tournament schedules and addresses of friends and cafés and decent rooms at reasonable prices.

Curl worked on his game until Thursday, when the two-day satellite began. Curl's horoscope in the morning paper said that the hard worker would reap rewards, and he did. He shot a 70 and was tied for second place with Johnny Jacobs and Roy Pace. The lead was held by a rabbit by the name of Billy Ziobro who had driven out from Jersey with the flu so bad he had to keep stopping to throw up.

Curl and Ziobro were paired the next day. There was almost no gallery following them. Ziobro's game was strong, but Mondays had taken some of the fight out of him. But today he was on his game, and he and Curl came to the eighteenth hole tied for first with Jacobs, who was in the clubhouse drinking a beer and looking for a card game. Ziobro put a wedge shot a foot from the pin, made the putt and took first prize away from Curl and Jacobs. But it was a good day for

Curl. He and Jacobs split second and third money and got $982 each.

Curl did a little shuffle out to his car, and he and Bonnie celebrated with some Kentucky Fried Chicken. The rates were so good at the Bayside that they decided to stay there and wait for Sunday to drive to Phoenix. Curl wouldn't have to qualify for the Phoenix Open, because he'd finished in the top twenty-five there the year before, another way to avoid Mondays. Curl would practice at Carlton Oaks Country Club all week, then drive to Phoenix early Sunday.

A hundred miles away, the LA Open had been going on for the big money. By Sunday the sports section of the LA *Times* reported that a man by the name of Funseth had a one-shot lead over a man name of Snead for the $30,000 first prize. In the streets of the city, people lost their jobs and their minds, they cheated each other, got cheated, stole, starved, cut each other up, and ran for public office.

But out at Riviera Country Club, about the worst thing that could happen would be to bogey a hole or not to be able to find a good parking place.

To the police directing traffic, the lines seemed endless. To the men in the Goodyear blimp, from up where they relayed shots down to the ABC production trailer, they looked like animal herds.

It was hectic in the ABC trailers. The producer was up on eighteen tower when he heard the word he was needed in the graphics trailer. He gulped down his Coke and headed carefully past the monitor set and the camera, off the wooden platform and down the steep steel steps. The tower was over thirty feet high and looked like the frame of an unfinished building. It wobbled slightly as the producer climbed down. He nodded to two of the men at the bottom who'd helped put the tower up on Monday and would take it down the next day when the tournament was over.

The Riviera members and the press and the people with the SPONSOR badges milled around the clubhouse area. They were the only ones allowed in the clubhouse. They had got those badges for donating money to the tournament, or from people who had, and they wore the badges like soldiers with the Croix de Guerre in a crowd of civilians who had never served . . .

The general admissions people hung around the hot-dog stands and the eighteenth green, sat under trees with picnic baskets, drank beer and joked and checked their pairing sheets to see who they ought to follow. Some wandered like dazed recruits trying to get back to their outfits.

The crowd marshals stationed around eighteen green listened to faint applause, which sounded like distant early-morning artillery fire. Soon it would all be moving their way and they would have to be ready.

The ice cream vendors were ready in their stands, the hot dog people had plenty of mustard, and the soda pop vendors were loaded with ice.

And the ABC producer was trying to find out where the last group was.

The last group was on the back nine, and Rod Funseth was still in the lead. The caddies around the practice green got up bets. "Funseth?" a black caddie said. "He can't do it. Don't hit but one bucket of balls a year. M-m-mother got in a sudden-death play-off there at Greensboro last year, and first thing he ask was how much second place worth."

Over in the pressroom, two touring reporters were making bets of their own, and taking critical looks at their free food. They were hoping that Funseth didn't win. Not that they had anything against the man.

They hardly knew him. It was just that Funseth wasn't flamboyant or eccentric or temperamental or funny. So they would have to write stories about what clubs he hit, where he made his birdies, what color shirt he had on.

"I'd just go with *soft-spoken, veteran Rod Funseth,"* the big, heavy one said as he eyed his prune Danish.

They had been hoping that Lee Trevino would win. Not that they liked him any better than Funseth. In fact, they were getting tired of Trevino's act. It was wearing thin. If he told a joke on the first tee and it didn't work, he'd try it again on the second tee. And they thought that Trevino *had one on* for the world. But he'd have so much to say, hit them with so much material, so many lines, that it would make it easy for them to write their stories without working too hard. But Trevino had let them down. He'd missed the cut.

The big reporter shook his head at his prune Danish. "This is a Class D breakfast. I'll be glad when we get to the Crosby and that big, free table."

As the final threesomes neared the televised holes, the socializers around the clubhouse could hear the cheers. They couldn't tell exactly where the cheers were coming from, but the biggest cheers of all, and the ones they never needed a program to figure out who they were for, came from the wildest of all of the herds the Goodyear blimp could see. They came from the mob trailing a man who, though in his mid-forties and struggling with his game and with himself, was still their god. It was Him. Arnie.

Palmer had shot 75–71–71, but he'd started playing like the Arnie of old on the back nine this final day. He'd have a big gallery if he was shooting 90. But after the crowds heard that he was making birdies, they came back like old lovers. Some of the socializers left the clubhouse, the picnickers left their shade trees, the marshals left their holes, and the reporters left what was left of their free food.

At this particular instant, he was in the woods, and someone from the crowd yelled, "Go for it, Arn." The man was obviously a dilletante. Arnie always goes for it. He would rather go through a brick wall than around it. He looked the shot over, looked toward the flag, said something to his caddie, then ripped a club out of the bag, took one last hard squint at the flag, hitched his pants and set himself over the ball. A father tugged at his son's sleeve and whispered, "Don't miss this."

Arnie hit one that came out of the deep rough, rose up and hooked in toward the hole. It hit, bit, and came rolling back three feet from the cup. The crowd stampeded for the green yelling, "CHARGE, ARNIE." "JUST LIKE OLD TIMES, ARNIE." "YOU CAN DO IT, ARNIE."

Near the eighteenth green, a heavy fellow with a large overbite, a Budweiser visor and an I'M JUST HERE FOR THE BEER T-shirt yelled out "Hey, Irma" so loud that Arnie had to step back from his putt. A thin, pale man pointed at the man and said, "Shut your mouth, you sonofabitch."

Arnie stepped back, squared his stance to the line and knocked it in for a 69.

The fans jammed their way around the scorer's tent just for a chance at an autograph or a nod or a hello or a smile.

Over on the other side of the green, Arnie's touring caddie, Ernest "Creamy" Carolan, slipped wearily through the ropes, unnoticed. He walked along holding his stomach. On the practice green the other caddies relaxed, their faces dirty, uniforms sweaty, tired, sore and petered out.

"Hey, whachoo shoot?" one of the black caddies asked.

"We shoot six-nine," Creamy said. "Should've shot sixty-six." He sat down next to Arnie's bag. Although sixty years old, he was in good shape, even better shape than Arnie. Creamy held his stomach. "The man's gonna give me ulcers." He pointed at his stomach. "He gets you *right here.*"

Creamy was Arnie's regular touring caddie, one of the caddies who travel on their own, working for one player exclusively or free-lancing week to week. Creamy had been with Palmer since 1969, but they were about ready to split.

Creamy looked toward the scorer's tent, where the crowd had Arnie surrounded. "A lot of goddam synthetic fans. Most of 'em don't even know what's goin' on." He turned to one of the other caddies. "Hell, I went to pro football when there was *nobody* there. Where were all those goddam clowns then? Hell, I can't help Palmer. You can't help a guy who won't listen to you. You can't pat him on the back and say 'Come on, pal. Let's go,' like you can a lot of guys. He won't listen, then he blames me for a bad shot. Today —today he walked by me like he didn't even know me. Hell, I'm the only real friend the guy's got out here but he doesn't even realize it."

Carroll West, a black touring caddie who spent twenty years in the Air Force and caddies to beef up his retirement pay, flipped his caddie badge up and caught it. He turned to his friend, a caddie they called "Golf Ball," and he said, "If Arnold treated me like he treats Creamy, me and him would get divorced. I'd ask him, 'Is there a creek down there on the sixth hole? Because if there is, that's where you'll find your sticks, *Bubba.*' "

Golf Ball took a long drink of beer from a cup and wiped his mouth. "Yeah, me too. He be diggin' those *AP's* out that muck."

The people working the big leaderboard near the

clubhouse had been working fast ever since the leaders teed off in the afternoon. The leaderboard had the names of the ten players who were leading the tournament, what holes they were on, and how many under par they were.

Rod Funseth had stayed on top all afternoon, and the name-droppers and socializers and picnickers all began to crowd toward eighteen green to watch the finish. Two people from Muncie, Indiana, were fighting their way up to the edge of the green. She was tired and wanted to leave, but he reminded her that they'd promised their neighbors they would try to get on the television. They got into position to wave and jump up and down if the camera made a pass at them. Perfectly intelligent and otherwise dignified people stood behind the taping of a TV interview with one of the golfers and made faces at the camera. Later, they would probably realize what they'd done and wish they hadn't done it. But right now, the red light was on, and federal judges and heirs to great fortunes waved their arms and stuck out their tongues . . .

In the pressroom, some of the reporters worked on Funseth leads. "Boyish-looking, soft-spoken, curly-haired veteran Rod Funseth . . ." some of them began.

Tom Place, a former Cleveland sportswriter who was the Tournament Players Division traveling information director, Xeroxed some of the rounds and scores and the money breakdown for the tournament. Then he set up a microphone for the top finishers to come in, go over their rounds hole by hole and shot by shot, and comment on how the course played. Because of the communications and the availability of the players for interviews, the reporters could get all of the material for their stories without ever having to leave the pressroom and watch the action . . .

. . . Which was drawing in toward eighteen now as

the final group came to the eighteenth tee. All of the cliques that had been following Palmer and Nicklaus and Johnny Miller and the others now came together down along eighteen fairway and followed Funseth in a little parade to the finish. Funseth had a three-shot lead coming down the stretch, and the people were as many as ten deep ringing the green. Others battled for position along the ropes on the fairway.

The caddies were crowded around the leader-board doing some last-minute betting on birdies and on second place.

"Y-y-you gotta find my range," one of the caddies said. "Five dollars won't do it. I wanna bet somethin' have *you* sweatin' and have *me* sweatin'."

Picnickers, walkers, gawkers and groupies came together in the big parade down eighteen. As Funseth neared the eighteenth green a sure winner, the crowd began what was at first only polite applause, which got louder and louder as he smiled, squinted and raised his putter in a victory salute. The TV camera on eighteen tower came in for a close-up and the marshals cleared the mob to make a path for Funseth to get to the pressroom.

When it was over, the crowd began to head back to their cars and the traffic jams of the outside world. The man in the Budweiser visor had apparently found Irma and was eating a Moon Pie in Palmer-like thrusts. People were making Walter Mitty passes at imaginary balls as they headed toward the parking lot.

The country club would go back to its members for another year, but the road show would head for Phoenix and a new opening next week. The players and wives said goodbye to one another and the caddies collected their salaries and found out where they could meet their cronies in Phoenix.

The Curl family was headed for Phoenix in the Mercury, $982 ahead of the rabbit, looking at the government-green subdivisional houses along the road out of Santee.

The tour was a grind, but it beat working in the Pak-A-Sak store or sorting mail or driving the bread route. The Pak-A-Sak managers probably made a decent salary, the Post Office had a good retirement plan, and bread route drivers were friends with everybody along their routes.

But they don't announce your arrival at the Pak-A-Sak store, and the bread route has no Hall of Fame.

The sun made long shadows on the clubhouse lawn at Riviera, and a warm front headed toward Phoenix. The door of the pressroom slammed and somebody yelled. Two caddies, one black and one white, ran side by side out of the pressroom, carrying sandwiches. A tournament official came out after them and told a security guard, "Those boys cleaned out the press food, goddammit." But the security guard was too old and/or tired to give much of a chase, and by the time he got up, the caddies had made it to the parking lot. Two other caddies were waiting in an old station wagon, and the driver was revving the motor so hard that the radiator fan squealed and blue smoke shot out of the tailpipes. The caddies with the food jumped in the back, and the driver gunned it while the man riding shotgun held on tight to six quarts of Pennzoil.

As they slid out of the parking lot the driver turned up the radio full blast. It was an old Chuck Berry song:

> *"I left my home in Norfolk, Virgin-ya,*
> *California on my mind.*
> *Straddled a Greyhound rollin' outta Raleigh*
> *And on across Care-o-line.*
> *Stopped in Charlotte, bypassed Black Hills,*

Never were a min-ute late.
We were ninety miles outta At-laaanta by sunup,
Rollin' outta Georgia state . . ."

The guard ran into the parking lot just in time to get a load of red dust and driveway gravel.

The season has started and the race is on.

2

From a Short Subject to a Spectacular

When the station wagon hit Phoenix, the six caddies inside were busted. The gas money had gone nearly as fast as the stolen sandwiches and the six quarts of Pennzoil. They found a caddie who'd had a good week and borrowed $20 from him and checked into the Motel Six as a twosome. They made two beds into four by putting mattresses on the floor, then made two more with rags, sleeping bags and blankets.

One of the white caddies came back from the El Rancho Market puffing a fat cigar. He rubbed his whiskers and started emptying the pockets of his baggy pants, tossing newly acquired items out on the car hood. Two packs of Roi Tan cigars, four packs of Juicy Fruit gum, a Mars bar and three Hersheys, some rolling papers and a can of Prince Albert tobacco. He reached into his other pocket. "Inflation?" —he worked the cigar around in his mouth—"Propaganda!" He pulled out a Zippo lighter and two packs of Gillette doubled-edged blades and rolled them out on the car hood like dice. "I'm tired of people knocking the country. If you're hungry, you fix a sandwich. If you need tobacco, you take it." He lifted up his shirt, bit down on the cigar and grinned. He had three packages of lunchmeat and the February issue of *Playboy* in his belt. "This is the greatest country in the world."

Rod Curl priced motel rooms up and down Van Buren Street and settled on one where the desk man kept a billy club. The room had two decent double beds and an old black-and-white Emerson that got most of the stations fairly clear. The toilet, however, hadn't been flushed from the time before.

The motels were even worse when Sam Snead and Johnny Bulla came through Phoenix for the first time. Back in 1934, when Paul Runyan led the money list with $6,767, the motels were called tourist courts, and the pro tour wasn't really a tour at all, just a few winter stops and mostly minor tournaments. The pro was a car-driving, cold-cuts eater and the tournaments were more of an adventure than a business— just something to do while the clubs were closed up north. The pro was a man with a club job who ran the shop, kept the clubs clean, the caddies in line and his mouth shut while he gave lessons to club members in a game that was as dull and conservative as they were.

Golf was more a social outing than a sport. The pro was nothing more than an employee who existed at the indulgence of the rich and wasn't even allowed to use the locker room or the dining facilities.

And if the employees wanted to take fool trips across country on their own time and play in these little outings, well, that was fine. As long as they were back there first thing in the spring.

And they always were.

They went for the good times and in hopes of meeting people who could put them on to nice business deals. The advantage to playing pro golf in those days was that nearly every amateur who played the game was rich or well connected. If the members liked you *and* if you could play, they might take up a collection for you to go out during the winter. The golf pro was far from being a star. The golfing hero of the era, in keeping with the order of things, was an amateur named Bobby Jones. The playing achievements of the professionals, with a few exceptions such as the U.S. Open and the British Open, went pretty much unnoticed, and served as back-page sports filler. In 1940, the year Jack Nicklaus was born, there was only $121,000 in tour prize money for the year. Still, in 1945, Byron Nelson won eleven tournaments in a row and earned more than $63,000. Nelson had been making a living at golf by taking excursions like the one he made down to South America in a DC-3 to play a month-long exhibition schedule for $1,500.

Today, if you went to Arnold Palmer and said "Fifteen hundred dollars," he'd think you wanted him to lend it to you.

After the war ended, life began to change in America. The wealth spread and the postwar economic boom enabled more people to join golf clubs and buy equipment, and, naturally, to become golf fans. By the 1950's people were beginning to notice pro golf, and if not to accept it, at least to no longer ignore it. Golf began to creep toward the front of the sports page. Newsreels of Eisenhower on the golf course or practicing putting on the practice green he'd had built on the lawn of the White House brought golf to national attention. And when Arnold Palmer and telecast golf came, people changed their minds about the game, and it became familiar to them.

Palmer's bold, wild game did not remind them of the Little Lord Fauntleroys who played golf because they were afraid to go out for football. The boys in the pizza parlors and bowling alleys across America figured if it was all right for this Palmer guy, it was okay for them, and they came out hacking—and buying $200 million worth of equipment and having three hundred new courses built each year to accommodate them. Golf in America grew to a billion-dollar budget—more than any other sport.

Today the successful touring pro in no way resembles the old club pro. He's an independent contractor, he doesn't run a club, and he really isn't beholden to anyone. He doesn't drive—he flies first-class or takes his private jet or hops by helicopter.

The big-name pros are showered with offers to stay in private homes. Car dealers come with free cars to drive. Restaurateurs open their doors to the stars. There are courtesy cars to pick the pros up at the airports and drive them to and from the golf course.

And where it stops, nobody seems to know. The course members plan and wait for a whole year, and all season long they watch the other tournaments on television. It's like waiting for the circus to hit town. Every tournament wants to outdo the other tournaments. The red carpet rolls out. There are police escorts with sirens and motorcycles.

A gate guard at Phoenix Country Club had never been to a tournament before. He had been listening to a golf pro cuss about a late courtesy car. "Hell, I wish *I* had me a courtesy car to work every day."

It is smart business to make the pros feel at home because the big names are needed to make the tournament a success, and royal treatment might just be what it takes to keep them coming back. But the pros begin to expect this kind of treatment wherever they go, and it's hard to get adjusted to normal life when they go back home. It's hard for them to stand in line at the grocery store or wait at the filling station for service. If you are treated like a king every week, it's not hard to start thinking that you are one.

An old golf bigot sits in the dining room at Phoenix sipping a daiquiri. He sighs, "It's the new money. My God, they're impressed with just anyone and they have *spoiled* our workers." It's the fault of a star-struck public. A British television announcer guesses that it's because we have no royalty in this country that we anoint movie stars and crown athletes.

And there wouldn't be much the athletes could do to change things, even if they wanted to. And as long as they are the recipients of the treatment, why would they want to? One young pro says, "If people are silly enough to do all those things for the players, hell, I won't turn it down. I might at first, but after a while, I'm probably going to be like everybody else."

Some resorts used to give comp rooms to the press, who could use the expense break, but now the rooms go to the exempt pros—not to the pros who could use the free rent, but, ironically, to those who would rather spend money to get the tax write-offs. The rabbits who could use free cars and free housing and free meals rarely get them, and the ones who don't need them can't find a place to hide.

In his world, the pro is indeed the most important person. And his world travels with him every week, all year long.

A policeman over on Ascension Street in New Orleans leaned against his squad car drinking a cold Nu-Grape. His uniform was soaked from the humidity. That day he'd been shot at, had a brick thrown at his car window, and had to fix a flat. A few minutes before, he had stopped a speeding car and given the driver a ticket. "He told me, 'Look, I'm with the golf tournament.'" The cop wiped off the top of his Nu-Grape with his sleeve. "I couldn't believe it. 'I'm one of the players,' he says. I told him that this was downtown New Orleans and he was goin' fifty in a thirty-five zone and he had better be in court before Monday at eight-thirty sharp or it would be his ass."

At the 1972 U.S. Open at Pebble Beach, three young men ran out on the eighteenth fairway the last day and chained themselves to the celebrated big tree in the middle of the fairway, and displayed a sign that said, "Stop the Bombing." A few people cheered. Most of the others were amused and thought it was rather entertaining. A few people were outraged. Joe Dey, the TPD (Tournament Players Division of the PGA) commissioner at the time, shook his umbrella at the three men and wanted to go out after them. The golfers played around the three protesters, who didn't try to interfere with the playing or to disturb anyone playing a shot. Later the young men said that their intention was only to point out to people that there were all these awful things happening in the world while they just went on about their frivolity, that while athletes got thousands of dollars just to play games, every time someone snapped his fingers, or every single second, someone in the world had just starved to death. They wondered why people would put all this money into games but not into programs to help people.

At the time, Al Barkow was the editor of *Golf Magazine* and he had been following Jack Nicklaus. He saw the young men locked to the tree. "In a way they're right. Why is there all this money in sports? And in a way they're wrong. People need an escape from all the problems in the world." It was like people in Mexico and South America building beautiful churches while they themselves lived on the edge of starvation. Maybe they needed those sanctuaries to carry on day after day.

Pro golf success is tabulated in dollars, even though the top sixty is figured from what the TPD calls an exemption-point list. The points are merely dollars won in 72-hole tournaments. What Fast Eddie Felson, the pool hustler in Walter Tevis' *The Hustler,* said applies to professional golf. "When it's all over, you count your money, and the guy with the most money is the best player." Not very romantic, but very realistic.

When Ernie Banks used to stride out of the dugout with his 31-ounce bat, nobody would say, "This guy's financially set." They would simply say, "There he is," and keep their eyes on the left-field seats.

But the pro golfer isn't a member of a team. He's an independent contractor. He doesn't travel in a team bus or stay in a team hotel. He doesn't have to worry about team morale or sacrificing for the sake of the team. He's his own team, and if he's making $100,000 a year out there, he doesn't really have to depend on anybody, and he can tell everybody to go to hell.

The old, proper, restrained upper-crust people who once ran the show have been replaced by the white-belt, white-shoe crowd, the franchise hamburger baron and the fertilizer magnate. Money is the undisputed ruler, the measuring stick, the first topic of discussion and the number one status symbol at golf tournaments.

The man in the dining room in Phoenix finished his daiquiri, assessed the service and tipped likewise. He sighed. "I'm afraid it's all gotten rather tacky."

Jerry Raskin is an advertising man who owns some property in Phoenix and makes the social scene. He doesn't play golf and he doesn't come to the tournament to watch the golf, and in that sense he is a typical Phoenix tournament-goer. He buys a couple of $50 sponsor badges from the Thunderbirds and makes the scene on Wednesday for the pro-am, then again on Saturday and sometimes on Sunday. "We come out here to see who's wearing what and who's screwing who these days. We come to visit and gossip, and most of the fans out here could care less that they're out there playing golf."

Raskin spends his day visiting with friends, finding out the latest social news. Cliques form near the clubhouse and around the hot-dog stands near the practice green. The women wear the latest outfits from the East Coast and parade around the clubhouse, visit, watch maybe one hole of golf or five minutes of putting practice, then head for the Bird's Nest.

The Bird's Nest is a tent with a band, next to the clubhouse. At about five o'clock the band starts as the sun goes down behind a leaderboard that few people pay much attention to.

The band plays, the gossip and the drinks get stronger. They talk about Calcutta pools.

For whatever arguments can be made that there is too much money directed toward games and not enough toward solving serious problems, it must be noted that tournament golf matches the $8 million in prize money with $8 million for charities from the tournament proceeds.

The Phoenix Open is run by a civic-minded group of young establishment and big-company strivers called the Thunderbirds. The Thunderbirds can best be described as a cross between the Chamber of Commerce and the Shriners. In between wild parties and minor sex scandals, the Thunderbirds work to bring excitement and culture to Phoenix. They even have their own costumes—velours pullover Nehru-type shirts and squash-blossom necklaces of Indian design. The Thunderbirds, like Kings of Kansas City, are big men in Phoenix, and their biggest week of the year is the Phoenix Open, when they have complete run of the limelight all week long. Dean Martin went to the Thunderbirds a few years ago and offered his name and services to the Phoenix Open before offering them to the Tucson Open. Martin's name and influence would've meant instant TV, celebrities, and consequently much, much more money for the charities the Thunderbirds oversee. But they turned him down and he went to Tucson, where the Dean Martin–Tucson Open has since been a great success.

There were some new condominiums going up over near Camelback Mountain. Somebody showed Jerry Raskin a copy of the Phoenix newspaper. There was a picture of policemen carrying a midget who had robbed a Phoenix bank.

Near the corner of the tent as dark spread out lightly across the high sky, two policemen helped a man out. The man was cumbersome and totally drunk. He couldn't talk, walk, or say his name. He couldn't tell the policemen where he lived. Finally the policemen sat him down just outside the tent, and two men told the police they knew the man and would take him home as soon as they finished their drinks. They left the man spread-eagled out on the patio.

And finally the college fight-song singers and the hard-core drunks began to leave too. The band quit playing. Two people were left, standing in front of the tent arguing. He was drunk and she was drunker. "I'm going home to an empty house," she said. She said it several times, and as she turned to walk away, fell into the bushes and spilled almost everything out of her purse.

It was somewhat like that every day, until the tournament ended.

Bruce Crampton won the tournament with twelve under par. One of the members saw the "−12" hanging on the leaderboard as the sun dropped low and made long shadows from the clubhouse. "Twelve under," he told his wife. "That's disgraceful. What'll the folks at Winged Foot think?"

The weather and the Emerson TV set at Curl's motel held up all week. He holed a shot from the fairway with a five-iron for an eagle to make the cut, shot 67–73–68–69, and unbeknownst to most of the folks at Phoenix, he made $465. He'd been pointing his game toward Tucson and he was excited. Tucson National was a long, wide-open golf course suited to his game and his pencil shot. The greens were big, the short froghair suited to his chipping game. He was ready. He knew that if he didn't drop dead he could make $5,000 there and at last have room to breathe.

He woke up early Monday morning. Semis shifted gears into the distance. Down the street a bottle broke. The low clouds that had moved in during the night were picking up the early downtown neon.

Tucson was two hours south.

3

Fools All
Settle to
the Bottom

Curl got caught flatfooted at Tucson by the rule book. There were so many rules in the game of golf that it was hard to keep track of them all. Sometimes those rules changed from one season to the next. One year, something that was legal the year before might be a two-shot penalty. The PGA decides that it would be a good idea to do something one way one year, and the next year they might decide that it wasn't such a good idea after all. There was a rule that Curl didn't know about, a new rule that said that if you wanted to play in a tournament, you had to sign up the Tuesday before, even though you might have made the cut at the previous tournament. The season before, it wasn't that way. Curl hadn't read his literature thoroughly, hadn't signed up for the Dean Martin–Tucson Open, and wouldn't be allowed to play in it. It was a long depressing ride out of town. He had tried to map this whole thing out in his mind. Tucson was supposed to be the big stopper. He'd figured on winning maybe $5,000, which would've given him the cash he needed to take the heat off.

If he didn't make $5,000 for the year, he would be subject to review by the TPD and would likely lose his player's card for lack of performance. If he got it going and made a run at the top sixty, and if he fell a few dollars short, he'd never forgive himself for Tucson. If you couldn't execute the shots, that was one thing. But if you beat yourself because of foolishness, that would be hard to swallow.

He didn't talk much to his wife as he drove toward California and the Monterey peninsula. There was a little tournament in Salinas called the Salad Bowl, a 36-hole two-day event played—for the sake of variety —on two golf courses. He could beat the courses with his long ball, and if he could make a few putts, he could beat the ducks who would be playing there. It was a private tournament and the prize money varied, depending on how much money the people there had raised. The previous year, Curl had tied for first place and had got $1,000.

Salinas was near Monterey, and the next tournament, the Bing Crosby Pro-Am, would be in Monterey. Curl hated to move all of his things from one motel to another, so they checked in at a motel in Monterey.

On Thursday morning he got up early, and while Bonnie stayed back at the motel with the kids, Curl headed for Salinas.

He needed some cigars and a cold 7-Up, so he stopped at the first little shopping center he came to. It was usually cool in Monterey, but the sun was warm for this time of year and this early in the morning. He sat out on the stoop of the little store, smoked a cigar and drank his 7-Up. The man who came up and sat down on the other side of the stoop had a liquor bottle. He cuddled the bottle close to him, as if he was guarding it. When he saw Curl looking, he held the bottle out.

"Betty Ann port," the man said. "Taste?"

Curl laughed. "Naw, I don't think I could handle that."

The man's eyes were yellow and hung low in the pouches. He lit a cigarette. "Doctors want me to quit the smokes. I been smokin' for about two hundred years. Can't seem to quit. I don't take the smoke down very far. Only about halfway. If I took it down all the way, I'd probably choke to death."

"You don't want to quit?"

"Yeah, well, what do those doctors know? Hell, my liver's gonna go long before my lungs. I'd be a fool to quit. What do you do for a living?"

"Play golf."

"Where you play it at?"

"All over the world."

"Well, how about *that.* Any money in it?"

"Not the way I do it."

The man edged in closer. "Say, you couldn't spare a buck or two for an old caddie, could you?" He'd been played pretty good by the man—not too tight and not too loose, and he could appreciate that. He reached into his pants pocket and dragged out two singles and started to put them in the man's shirt pocket, then he hesitated. "Promise you won't spend it on soup?"

As Curl drove toward Salinas he thought about that man. You always think you're about to the bottom, then you see that the bottom is a lot deeper than you thought.

Curl was playing, the first day, at Salinas Country Club. Since he'd tied for first the year before, the few people there knew him, would say hello and point him out. He got a bucket of balls and went down to the end of the practice area.

He walked out and paced off fifty yards and marked the spot by putting a stick into the ground. Because his stride was short, he had to walk ten

strides for nine yards. He spread the balls out next to
him and pulled out a wedge and started hitting easy
little shots toward the stick. After he'd hit about a
dozen balls, a man in a visor came up and started
watching him. He liked to have people around the
practice tee while he was hitting. At the tournaments,
he didn't get many galleries unless he was close to the
lead the last two days, or paired the last two days with
Nicklaus or Palmer. Even then, people weren't there
to watch him.

Curl hit a few shots and talked to the man, who,
like Curl, liked to hunt. The man had hunted deer but
he had never hunted elk. They talked on and on about
thirty-ought-six rifles and what the best ammunition
was for mule deer.

The man pointed to a sign over near the far side of
the clubhouse. "You think you could hit that sign with
a twenty-two?" the man said.

Curl drew a bead with his wedge. "I could hit that
o in GOLF."

"You doing any good on the tour?" the man said.

Curl sat down and lit a cigar, turning his back to
the breeze so the match wouldn't go out. "I'm gettin'
bounced around like a cue ball. About like those deer.
Run or get killed. I figure in two or three years, if I'm
alive out here, I'll be where I want to be. If I don't, I
can always hunt deer."

Curl put his wedge down to get an idea of where
he was aiming, to see if his feet were lined up right.
He showed the man what it was he was doing. "Amateurs just walk up and hit it. They depend too much
on talent. You got to have technique too." He showed
the man how to line the club face to the target, then
stand at the same angle as the club. "That way, you're
right on the money."

"That really helps?"

"That's the shot little guys have to have. That's the

shot you got to have to make birdies on those par fives. That's the shot you got to have if you miss a green. All the pros work on that fifty-yard shot. Watch Trevino or Gary Player. That shot I hit on the stick, that was too hard. I need to land it about three of four feet short. If it bites, I'm in tight. If it doesn't, I might be four of five feet on the other side of the cup."

He took the man over to the practice green and paced off fifty yards. "You just open your stance way up. It's just like tossing a ball underhand. You get way down on it and toss it up there." He hit one that took off toward the pin on the practice green. He threw a right cross out toward the stick as the ball came down, then pulled back hard as it hit and bit a foot from the pin.

He hit the whole bucket of balls at the green. "Damn, I must have forty birdies in there." They went back over to the practice area.

He looked out at the 150 sign. "See that zero on the one-fifty marker?" The man nodded. Curl hit a shot that started out to the right and drew in toward the sign and went just over the "5" in the 150. "Missed." He hooked another shot that drew in faster and hit right in front of the zero. The man looked amazed. Curl grinned. "If I could just do that when the heat's on."

"That's almost magic."

Curl laughed. "And I'm not even one of the top hundred players."

"Maybe you'll get there."

"It's sure taking a long time. A lot of it rides on the next month or two. If I can make some cash and get me a little cushion, I can gamble a little and go for those birdies. And if I can do that, I can make a run at the top sixty. And if I can do that—I can win. And if I win one . . ."

He pulled out his driver and asked the man if he

had a pencil. "I got a Flair pen," the man said.

"Let me use it. I won't break it. If I do, I'll buy you another one." He stuck the pen in the ground and put a ball on it. He got set, took the club back and caught it dead solid. As the ball took off, the man squinted. When it rose, he got up on his feet. The ball rose up, up, and it kept going.

"That's outta here," the man said. "My God. How'd you do that? Where'd you learn that?" The man shook his head. "I've never seen anybody forward press and throw those hips out there like you do. I just can't believe you can hit a ball that far. Where's that power coming from?"

"I don't know," Curl said. "I really don't. But I know this." He stuck the Flair pen back in the man's shirt pocket. "If I learn to hit that ball dead straight before I starve, I might rule the world."

It was time for him to get ready to tee off.

He birdied the third hole, then bogied, then birdied again. He made an eight-footer for a par on the ninth hole and turned the corner even-par. He hit the next par-five with a driver and a long iron and two-putted for a birdie. He bogied the next hole out of the rough, then birdied sixteen and seventeen and rimmed one on eighteen. He was in with a 69, two shots off the lead.

The next day's round was out at Coral de Terra. Curl had a little gallery of about ten people. He turned the corner in even-par, and he had a chance for a good check. He bogied ten, birdied eleven, bogied twelve and birdied thirteen. He parred all the way to eighteen. At eighteen tee someone told him that he needed a birdie to win. It was a nice feeling, because about the worst he could do was tie.

He didn't take any time. He had 153 to the center of the green, 156 to the pin. He took out a seven-iron, stepped up, hit the shot and sent it dead at the flag. It touched down ten feet short of the pin and bit hard. He was about eight feet from the hole. He lined it up. It was straight. And it was uphill. He stroked it, it headed for the cup, and he raised both arms over his head. Dead center. He didn't even know what the first prize was, but it turned out to be a $1,500 check. He folded it carefully and thanked the tournament officials and the people from the club.

That $1,500 was the break he needed. He could breathe. Three thousand in three weeks. He'd felt pretty bad about not being able to play at Tucson, but he knew it would've taken a high finish and a lot of luck to win as much as he'd already made in two days.

They went out and ate steak dinners that night. It wouldn't be such a hard wait in Monterey now.

4

"Makeup!"

Bing Crosby didn't invent golf until 1937. He did it in much the same way that Don Ameche invented the telephone. More or less by accident. In the thirties, Crosby was nearing the summit of his popularity. He was a horse player and a golfer on the side, and he lived near Del Mar Race Track about twenty miles north of San Diego. In 1937, when he invited some show-business pals and some pro golfers he'd come to know to play some golf and have a barbeque at nearby Rancho Sante Fe, he didn't realize that right there, for pro golf, the blue of the night had met the gold of the day.

But nobody was looking beyond that next barbequed rib. They played eighteen, ate the barbeque, had some entertainment, drank, joked and decided to do it again the next year. Sam Snead was the low pro with a 68, and Crosby took the prize money from his own pocket.

The next year they hyped it with a little radio and made a movie with some comedians in it, and sold it

38

to United Artists as a short subject. In 1943 the tournament was canceled because of the war, and Crosby and Bob Hope took their road show out and sold millions of dollars in war bonds through their golf exhibitions. In 1947 Crosby got the tournament going again. He'd made a deal with Del Monte Properties to play the tournament on their three great courses—Pebble Beach, Spyglass Hill and Cypress Point—up around Carmel Bay.

The Crosby tournament is played on the three courses to give the golfers a chance to test their skills on each course, and to add some variety to the spectating.

In 1973 the Crosby was the highest-ranked golf telecast on the Nielsen rating list, the Bob Hope Desert Classic was second, the Andy Williams–San Diego Open was third, then came the U. S. Open and the Masters. In fact, the 1972 Crosby in January drew more fans to Pebble Beach than the U. S. Open played there the following June.

Crosby is the first to admit that his galleries come mostly to see the stars. They want tinsel, not great shots. They want Efrem Zimbalist, Jr., they want Ray Bolger, Phil Harris and Joe DiMaggio. And if Palmer skulls a couple or whistles a few from the traps, even his loyal army drifts over to watch Jack Lemmon or somebody make twelve on the last hole.

When TV came, Crosby went after all the names he could get. The more the better. He was helping pro golf, having a good time himself, and contributing millions of dollars to charities.

The celebrity format is the key to the future success of professional golf, and many of the lesser-known tournaments have been trying to get celebrities of their own. Celebrities are flown in on expenses, plus very often a nice sum of under-the-table money which may be given back to the tournament as a donation and a tax write-off. They are flown in to play in the Wednesday pro-ams, to help attract the stargazers to the gates.

In the early 1960's, Bob Hope got involved in the Palm Springs Desert Classic, which was floundering, and it became an instant success. Andy Williams got involved with the dying San Diego Open, got TV there, and made it a successful tournament. Dean Martin went with Tucson, Jackie Gleason went with the new Inverrary Classic in Fort Lauderdale, Florida, an instant success. Glen Campbell joined forces with the LA Open, Danny Thomas with the Memphis Open, and Sammy Davis, Jr., with the Hartford Open.

One of the lesser-known tournaments, the Quad Cities Open, tried several celebrities with no success. They even tried Jimmy Dean, but he didn't have the time, and—fortunately or unfortunately, depending on your point of view—the Jimmy Dean Pure Pork Sausage Open never became a reality.

In the middle of the Danny Thomas Memphis Classic, Danny Thomas makes a plea for money for the children's hospital the tournament benefits. In one long moment he pauses, stares into the camera, eyes watering, voice cracking, and he says, "Please friends . . . I can't do it *all* myself." And there, in a way, you have it.

The normal weather forecast at the Crosby is as depressing as news from Southeast Asia. But the gallery veterans welcome it like an old buddy. It's tradition, a challenge, their duty, to brave the cold rain and sleet.

One fellow was huddled up against the trees in a driving rain near the eighteenth at Spyglass. He was wearing a parka and holding both ears. "I've seen worse," he kept saying. "I've seen worse."

No matter what the weather, people will come to

star-gaze, and the Crosby crawls with celebrities from the entertainment world. You might see James Garner over on the practice green, Dean Martin walking into the lodge, George Blanda and Jack Kramer joking in the bar, Peter Falk and Jack Lemmon hitting shags.

Much of the Hollywood glamour has gone. To Sheila Graham, Hollywood has become "a scruffy place full of television." But to those of us who grew up in the lackluster of boring small towns, Hollywood the place couldn't be separated from the Hollywood that existed only on the silver screen and was an escape from the bleak winters and the honky-tonk joints where early-morning drinkers were mean by noon.

Bob Newhart is not Clark Gable, but he'll do.

The Crosby format is pro-amateur.

The pros and amateurs are teamed together in a pro-am. Those amateurs who can afford anywhere from $500 to $1,500, depending on the tournament, and who can get in, get their chance to tee it up for eighteen holes with a pro in actual competition.

Each pro has usually three amateur partners. The amateurs get their handicaps, depending upon how poorly they play, up to a one-stroke spot per hole. In the team score that is kept, the pro plays scratch, without a spot. The amateurs get spots on the toughest holes. If a player is a 10-handicapper, he gets a stroke on each of the ten toughest holes. If the pro gets a *4* on a hole and his partners don't do better with their spot, then a *4* is recorded as their best-ball score for the hole. If an amateur with a spot on that hole gets a *4,* then a *3* is recorded as their best-ball score for the hole. The team score is kept hole by hole, then totaled up, and the pros with the low team score get prizes usually from $500 for first down to $100 for fifth.

The pros keep their individual scores and get equal prize money for the five low rounds of the day. The pro-ams are usually played on Wednesdays, the day before the tournaments officially begin.

Some of the pros dread the pro-ams, consider it hard work playing with duffers who keep them from concentrating on their own games. But most of the pros like the pro-ams. It gives them a chance to meet some people who might do them some long-range financial good. It gives them a chance to relax, to play an extra practice round, to double-check their yardages.

The amateurs are sometimes a lot more serious about the pro-ams. They have waited for weeks and months for this one day, this one round. The've taken crash lessons, beat balls, read instruction books, and worked very hard on their games. Sometimes too hard. They come to the first tee not only overdressed but overworked. Scared. Knees knocking. In need of a drink. Hardly able to take the club back.

The amateurs' friends and families are there to watch and cheer them on. The amateurs have paid for eighteen holes and a name to drop. They'll be the envy of some of their fellow members. And that pro will be their pro forever. They'll follow him through the sports pages for the rest of his career. And they'll follow him the rest of the week. "My drive was right there," they'll tell their friends. "I wanted to hit a wood, but Arnie talked me into a two-iron."

The pro-am money goes toward paying the purse. Because the tournaments are connected with charity work, the money can be written off the income tax. Some amateurs are sponsored by companies who want their names on the sponsor boards near the clubhouse, want the write-off, and want to reward their executives and employees with a round of golf with one of the touring pros.

The Crosby is a four-day pro-am, which is one of the things that make it unique. For their money—Crosby has kept it down to $600—the amateurs get to play three days with a different pro each day. If their team makes the cut, they get to play the fourth day.

At the very same time, the Crosby is an official tournament for the pros, using their 72-hole scores just as they would at a regular tournament. So what the amateur is doing is playing alongside the pros while the tournament is in actual progress, which can be compared in a way with climbing into the ring alongside Ali for his fight with Foreman, or being in center field at Yankee Stadium while the game is actually going on.

There were thirty-five team prizes at the Crosby, from $3,500 down to $100, but the pros were looking toward that $35,000 individual prize.

The amateurs have to be invited by Bing, and sometimes have to get on a waiting list of movie people, personalities from other sports, people from big business, and Bing's personal friends.

The pros get into the Crosby the same way they get into the other tournaments, which meant that Rod Curl had to qualify. He shot 72 and got one of the twenty-eight spots left open. He was to play Spyglass the first day, then Pebble Beach the next, then Cypress Point the third day. The cut would be made after the third day, then all of the action would be at Pebble Beach. The courses were all close together, and the fans could see action on all three in one day. The 54-hole cut gave every pro and amateur a chance to play each course.

The network cameras would be on Pebble Beach, so the scheduling of the rounds was such that the big-name pros and famous amateurs played Pebble Beach on Saturday, the first day of the telecast.

There were big turnouts even for the practice

rounds on Tuesday and Wednesday. The movie stars were dressed like golfers, and the fans were dressed like movie stars.

Early Thursday morning the sun broke through the groves of trees in the Del Monte Forest and the white sand dunes picked up the reflections off the ocean. And then the heavy clouds came rolling in off the ocean, and before noon it was raining.

Some of the fans huddled under trees arguing about which storm was worse than the last one. Only the weak, sick and faint of heart let the rain get them down. The wind blew and the waves crashed against the jagged rocks near the eighteenth at Pebble Beach. The deer that had been grazing on the fairways at Cypress Point headed for cover.

Play that first day was agonizingly slow. It was especially slow around the eighteenth green, where the galleries were. One amateur was thirty-two over par and asking for a ruling.

Several pros complained to the tournament committee about the slow pace. "It's the damn amateurs," one pro said. "If they can't help the team on a hole, they ought to pick it up and put it in their pocket and try again on the next hole."

Another pro was wringing out his socks. "For six hundred bucks, they can hit it as many goddam times as they want."

Dave Hill was rubbing down his club grips with gasoline to make them tacky. "You wait till the last two days. When the teams who are out of it start getting drunk and screwing off while you're trying to win the tournament. That's when it's a zoo."

The fans had different problems. They had to decide whether to follow a big-name pro with an obscure amateur or an obscure pro with a famous celebrity. Jack Lemmon and Robert Stack with Bob Eastwood and Rocky Thompson? Or Jack Nicklaus with Robert Hoag?

A door-to-door salesman argued with his wife. She wanted to see Mac Davis over at Spyglass, but he was afraid he'd miss Nicklaus coming in on Cypress. He asked a Jesuit priest he'd met for advice, and the priest gave him guidance. He told him to pick up his portable seat and follow Johnny Jacobs and Ray Floyd playing with Efrem Zimbalist, Jr., and Clint Eastwood, which would leave plenty of time to see Nicklaus finish. It was divinely inspired guidance, and the salesman followed it.

Rod Curl shot 74, and was eight shots off the lead, which was held by Billy Casper. Casper sat in the pressroom telling reporters that he was surprised he played so well because his back had been bothering him. He said he would win if the Lord was willing. Casper would never have said that before he met his wife and converted to Mormonism. Now, 10 percent of his winnings—with one intermediate stop at the Church of Jesus Christ of Latter-day Saints—went straight to God.

Some of the more worldly people at that Crosby went to squander some of their 10 percent in the clubhouse bar at the Del Monte Lodge. The drinking and name-dropping went long into the afternoon. A woman stood near the entrance of the bar, looking very aloof. She fixed one of her earrings and told the woman with her, "This is a public course."

"You *mean,*" her friend said, "that they let the citizens play here?"

That night the Hollywood crowd celebrated. The fires in the lodge were banked and lit and banked again. The houses around the rich little city of Monterey were lit with hard and soft music, the people on Cannery Row were lit with hard and soft liquor.

And on Friday, the rain stopped and it was clear. Rod Curl shot 75 and was in danger of missing the cut. He was sixteen shots off Billy Casper's lead. Casper, *somewhat* concerned about the ways of the world, was trying to take off some excess fat, drinking a diet cola in the pressroom. While outside on the steps, Orville Moody, the man in second place, was talking with his caddie. Orville had been a career army non-com who surprised everybody, even himself, by winning the 1969 U. S. Open. Since then, however, times had been hard.

Most of the other pros felt sorry for Orville because he was such a great shot-maker and such a poor putter. He hadn't capitalized on his Open win. He made $79,000 the year he won the Open, then began to slide to $50,000, $25,000, then to just $13,000 in 1972. The only way he survived in '72 was by going out late in the fall onto one of the mini-tours in Texas where you put up your own cash for prize money, then try to win everybody else's. Now he was clawing his way back. As they sat on the steps drinking Cokes, Orville told his caddie, "Sam, if I have a good year, I'll buy you a new car."

Sam was confident. "It will be a blue Dodge."

Some people thought that Casper had it all wrapped up. But not the smart money, and the smart money is very often in the caddie shack. Odds-maker Jimmy the Greek once said that if they rematched David and Goliath, the smart money would still be on the big man.

And the big man was most certainly Jack Nicklaus, who was seven shots back, but hardly out of it. If Nicklaus barely makes the cut, he's still a threat to win. The other players are intimidated just by his presence. "Do the other players worry when Nicklaus is four or five shots back?" a reporter asked John Jacobs.

"Hell, no," Jacobs said. "You worry about Jack when you see him signing up for the tournament."

Nicklaus seemed luckier than most players, but it was because he was always there when the opportunities arose. He was like a good poker player, waiting for the other players to make mistakes until the cards started coming his way.

Pete Brown and Curtis Sifford were watching the tournament on the TV set in the locker room. As the tournament play ended for the day, Nicklaus was five shots back of Moody, who'd taken the lead.

"Orville might leave the back door open," Sifford said.

"Jack can come in any door," Brown said.

"If I was the commissioner," Sifford said, "I'd give Jack a handicap. I'd start him four-over on the first tee."

Brown thought about it. "Doesn't matter. He'd win anyway."

William Price Fox said that the nickname "Golden Bear" fits Jack Nicklaus like "a blue tutu and pink pantyhose," because bears are "big sleepy creatures known for their low comedy of pushing over trash cans and hibernating most of the winter. A bear can survive on roots and berries. Nicklaus is a meat-eater."

What Jack Nicklaus is, is the best player ever, in the history of the game. Even the old die-hards give him the edge over Hogan and Snead. The immortal Bobby Jones once watched as Nicklaus made mockery out of par, and he said, "He plays a game unfamiliar to us all."

Today, Nicklaus is popular and respected, but it wasn't always that way.

And after his first season, after defeating everybody's hero Arnold Palmer in a play-off for the U. S. Open championship, practically in Arnie's backyard, he was hated. Nicklaus was shy, but people interpreted it as cold. He had such great concentration that he never paid the kind of attention to the galleries that Arnie did. And he looked like the neighborhood bully, the kid who sat in the front row, always raised his hand, always had the right answers.

But worst of all, he was fat. Fatties are okay for comic relief, as Andy Devines bouncing in the saddles, holding their hats and yelling, "Wait for me, Wild Bill." But they won't do as heroes.

Arnie was exciting; Jack was perfect, too perfect. He hit too many fairways, missed too few putts. Arnie might birdie a par-five without ever being in the fairway. Jack would simply hit the green in two and two-putt for his birdie. We weren't looking for that. We wanted surprises.

Arnie was more like one of the boys. Nicklaus didn't go in for locker-room horseplay. He wouldn't stay all day and joke with the reporters. If he was in an interview, he'd keep a close eye on his watch. He was honest, too honest with his answers—he came off cocky. A cocky, fat kid, cold as steel.

Nicklaus suffered through a lot of abuse—or rather, had to concentrate through it. The press didn't care for him, the fans called him "Fat Jack" and yelled at him to miss those little putts. He was the villain during the sixties.

And then two things happened. Arnie quit winning, and Jack lost weight. He let his hair grow, became a little more conscious of the public and the press. And meanwhile won more major championships than any player who'd ever lived. Dominated the game.

Now Nicklaus looks the part of a hero. Blond, steely-eyed and square-jawed, smiling at the galleries, walking down the center of the fairway in long strides to cheers instead of jeers. It took a physical change for Nicklaus to be accepted by the public, for the public to look deep enough into the man to see that he was not at all cold, but considerate, compassionate and the perfect model of his boyhood idol,

Bobby Jones the gentleman golfer.

If Nicklaus shoots 80, he will simply say, "It's the best I could've done under the conditions, the way I played." Gracious in victory, more gracious in defeat. Never a complaint, never an excuse.

And never much patience for the hard commerce of the sport. You will never see Nicklaus jumping up and down on a mattress or singing soda-pop jingles. Early in his career, when he'd won the Bob Hope Desert Classic, he was being congratulated by a TV commentator who decided to use Nicklaus to plug the car company sponsoring the telecast. "Yes, Jack," the commentator said, "and you also won this BRAND-NEW CAR." Nicklaus said, "Yeah, right," and moved quickly out of camera view.

Arnie's life was golf. He was not a reader, except perhaps for the golf magazines and maybe *Classic Comics.* Arnie was a jock. Nicklaus is a deeper thinker, concerned about the the condition of the world, the first to say that athletes get too much money, that our priorities aren't what they should be.

As Nicklaus walked down the first fairway that last day at the Crosby a woman tugged at her husband's sleeve. "He looks handsome now that he's slimmed down." Nicklaus wasn't concerned about the galleries right then. He was thinking about his game and the lead held by Orville Moody.

And Moody's thoughts must have been on Nicklaus. By the time Nicklaus made the turn at the ninth hole the lead had been cut from five shots to two.

A reporter walked along talking about Nicklaus. "To think of all of the millions of people who've played this game and the millions who've been pretty good at it. And the thousands who were so good at it that they were like magicians. And then that there's this one guy who's better than anyone who's ever picked up a club . . . and that he's right out there now, walking down the fairway . . ." The reporter had a picture of Nicklaus sitting at a table talking to Palmer. "Someday," he said, "when this picture yellows, people will look at it the way you might look at a picture of Milton talking to Shakespeare at the Mermaid Tavern."

Nicklaus was handling the fairways and the greens. He is awesome power and pinpoint precision, and he is also one of the best putters in the world, maybe the best on fast greens. In the 1962 Open win over Palmer, in five rounds on monstrous greens as fast as marble tabletops, Nicklaus three-putted only once.

Nicklaus finished the round with a 71, making up four shots on Moody, and tied for second with Ray Floyd. He was still in it and he knew it. Moody had yet to play the eighteenth hole, a par-five. Orville hit two good shots, then put his third shot on the green about twenty-five feet away. But he three-putted, and there would be a sudden-death play-off.

Nicklaus felt sorry for Orville, but there would be no pity during the sudden-death play-off. "A golf tournament is seventy-two holes. You have to make a putt at every hole, including the last one," he said. "I missed my share of putts. Everybody did."

They would start the sudden-death play-off on the fifteenth hole, and Nicklaus the family man was now Nicklaus the killer. As they stood on the fifteenth tee, Nicklaus stared at the green. He wasn't smiling, he wasn't joking.

Standing on that fifteenth tee with Nicklaus that day, Orville Moody and Raymond Floyd must have felt crowded, like the fellow who fought Sugar Ray Robinson, and when they finally woke him up after round number one, all he could say was, "I didn't know the ring could be that small."

On the first play-off hole, the greatest player who

ever lived lined up a birdie putt, knocked it in to win the tournament.

The Bing Crosby National Pro-Am was over, another notch for Nicklaus, heading for the center place in the Hall of Fame.

One rabbit joked in the locker room, "I wonder how he knew Orville was going to shoot seventy-six?"

The tournament was over, the stars were leaving, and in the bar in the lodge, some joker yelled, "CUT. PRINT IT."

While outside in the parking lot, a man who'd seen every star was drinking port wine from a flask. He had been on three weeks of almost heroic drinking that had covered three states, and all he could say at this stage was, "Nothin' like this in Logan, Utah."

Rod Curl made only $425 for the week, but he would be in the next tournament. He talked to another rabbit outside the locker room at Pebble Beach. They had watched the play-off on the locker-room TV. The other rabbit was talking about Nicklaus. "All that talent and *luck* besides. It isn't fair. It just isn't *fair.*"

It wasn't fair.

It never is.

5

Arnie!

The San Jacinto Mountains of the Southern California desert were worlds away from the blue peaks of Mount Olympus, where, according to mythology, the golden-headed heroes of ancient Greece, having died in the flower of their youth, loved and renowned, sit on ivory thrones with eagles at their feet.

Arnold Palmer, God of Golf, sat lacing his shoes in the locker room at Indian Wells Country Club before the first round of the Bob Hope Desert Classic. Arnold Palmer, greater than great, bigger than life, killed robbers and evil beasts and saved people in the ocean.

When Arnold Daniel Palmer was a boy, the son of a Pennsylvania steel-town club pro, he was forbidden by his father to mix socially with members or their children, and he'd play lonely rounds of golf on days when nobody was around. Sometimes when he'd make a putt, he'd announce to the trees, "Arnold Palmer of Latrobe, Pennsylvania, is the new champion."

And soon he was.

In 1954, at the age of twenty-four, he won the U.S. Amateur championship, quit selling paint and went on tour. He won tournaments the first few seasons, but it was 1960 that brought him into the spotlight. Palmer won the 1960 Masters in the fashion that was to typify his more than sixty wins, mark him as the most exciting player ever, bring him world-wide fame and an unforgettable name. When it looked as if all was lost, Palmer birdied the last few holes and won the 1960 Masters. A few months later, when they were still talking about that Masters, Palmer went into the last round of the U.S. Open at Cherry Hills in Denver in fifteenth place, seven shots back of the leader. Palmer shot a 30 on the front side, which was to be labeled by some experts as the greatest nine holes of golf ever played, shot a total of 65, and won the tournament by two shots.

Palmer's style was to win on the last few holes, taking radical chances, pulling off the impossible. And since the last few holes were always the ones televised, the viewers were treated to the *Perils of Pauline.* Even when Palmer lost, he would do it in a dramatic fashion.

There were experts who called his style courageous, others who said it was bravado. Golf had been a game where you played precision, not power; you thought your way around, you didn't bull your way through. But there was one thing they agreed about— it was more fun watching Palmer lose than watching the rest of them win.

Every week it was like Bronco Billy Anderson, World's Bravest Cowboy, pinned down behind the rocks and running low on ammo. If you were to say "Charge" to someone before 1960, they would probably immediately have thought of Teddy Roosevelt up San Juan Hill. But today, they would think of Arnold Palmer, hitching his pants, puffing on his cigarette, pacing, flipping the cigarette and going for broke. Palmer's price went up faster than IBM stock in the 1960's. In 1960 he won eight tournaments and doubled what the second-place money-winner made for the year. There would be the Arnold Palmer Golf Company, the Arnold Palmer Dry Cleaners, Arnold Palmer shirts, shoes, hats, sportcoats, dress suits, golf bags, putting courses, driving ranges, rain gear, Cadillac dealership, and teahouses in Japan.

Arnold Palmer was the greatest thing that had ever happened to golf. He generated tremendous interest in the game, and the purses went up and up and up, from a half million when he started to eight million today.

Palmer's heroics would earn him the title of Athlete of the Decade in the 1960's.

But time passed, the dogwood blooms dropped, and the hero was smoking his last cigarette. It was a hard fate for a hero—the fans still screaming for him and he unable to deliver. He told his mother that a dish his wife cooked didn't taste as good as when his mother cooked it the same way back when he was a kid. "You were hungrier then," she said.

Palmer had thought about retirement a lot lately. He'd begun to wonder whether he'd ever win a tournament again. But after a career in the spotlight, it was hard for him to simply walk away from all of it.

"Saw that man in Dallas once," a caddie said. "Biggest rainstorm I've seen before or since. Arnie come out on a balcony, no umbrella. Stayed there in the rain signing autographs and shaking hands and talking to fans and they wouldn't leave either. He must've stayed out there in the rain like that for an hour."

Watching Palmer shoot 78's and miss cuts is like

watching Sugar Ray Robinson, late in his career, lose to fighters who couldn't have lasted a round with him in his prime.

They say he could win if he changed his style, started playing precision, playing safe. But Palmer would rather lose than play safe and win. He lost one U.S. Open with a seven-shot lead with just nine holes to go. Palmer never protected his leads. To Arnie, that would've been the coward's way out. He lost a lot of tournaments with double-bogies and triple-bogies playing with abandon down the stretch. But he won the devotion of the masses, and he gets mail delivered to him even though it's addressed:

Arnold Palmer
Somewhere In Pennsylvania

And at a recent tournament a man on a loudspeaker announced the players as they came to the first tee. Names, hometowns, winnings for the year, the career, best finishes in major tournaments and so on. But when he saw it was Arnie on the tee, he put his script aside and announced, *"Arnold Palmer . . . He's known throughout the world."*

Going into the Bob Hope Desert Classic, the God of Golf hadn't won in a year and a half.

He went out and shot 71 that first round and signed autographs until a man in a cart with a sign on it that said "PGA PRESS" came to rescue him. "A couple more," Arnie told the man. "You drove down here from San Francisco," he said to one lady, squeezing her hand lightly. "I sure hope I didn't disappoint you."

His caddie said, "You think June Haver had charm? Hah! You haven't seen anything. He's the only player I've ever seen who'll sign autographs during a round no matter what."

*The man in the "PGA PRESS" cart drove Palmer
toward the press tent.*

The love affair between Palmer and the press
started early in his career. He gave them great stories
with his style of play, but he had time for them too.
A man who wants to be famous has to have a soft spot
for the men who are getting him there. Once, at Phoenix, the reporters were asking him about his round
when someone came up to him and reminded him
that he had a very important flight to catch. "Cancel
the reservation," he said. "I haven't spent enough
time with these guys."

One of the reporters who was around the tour in
the sixties said, "Arnie would come into the press tent
no matter what. After he lost that seven-shot lead to
Casper in the Open, he came in and talked with the
reporters for as long as they wanted, even though he
must've been in the worst pain of his whole life."

*Palmer talked with reporters in the press tent
about his opening round in the Hope Classic. He was
five shots behind Jack Nicklaus's 66, but the Hope was
a 90-hole tournament, the longest on the tour. Palmer
said Yes, he had a good chance, and No, five shots
wasn't that big a lead with that many holes, even
though it was Nicklaus who held it.*

It was the presence of Jack Nicklaus that was
partly responsible for Palmer's slide from the top. In
1962, after Palmer had won the Masters, they were
talking about a modern version of the "grand slam,"
which would mean winning the Masters, the U. S.
Open, the British Open and the PGA Championship.
The Open was at Oakmont, Pennsylvania, almost in
Arnie's backyard. Nobody played better than Palmer
—tee to green—but he was pressing for the home fans

and his great putting stroke abandoned him. He
three-putted ten times, and at the end of four rounds,
he was tied with a magnificent rookie named Nicklaus. Nicklaus beat Palmer 71–74 in a head-to-head
play-off the next day, and for the first time Palmer
realized that he could be beat. That loss planted a
little seed of doubt in Palmer's mind, a seed that grew.
The next year, Palmer lost another Open, to Julius
Boros, again in a play-off.

Time did the rest. The once supreme confidence
began to slip away.

*A caddie watched him miss a short putt that sec-
ond day at the Hope. "Hole used to be scared of him.
He'd look at it and the hole got scared. Now he's
scared of the hole. The hole knows it too."*

*But he started making those little putts that sec-
ond day, and before that day was over he had shot a
66, and it was just like old times for the galleries.*

The big shoulders, the arms like a steelworker's,
the hands as big as brickbats. To the fans who got
their first look at the game through Palmer, he didn't
look like the prissies they'd associated with the game.
He looked more like somebody who'd just jumped
down off a truck. It was in 1958 at the Masters that an
Augusta reporter coined the term "Arnie's Army."
Palmer's facial expressions gave away his emotions.
The fans looked at him and he looked as if he needed
their help—and maybe he did. "GO GET 'EM, AR-
NIE." "YOU CAN DO IT, ARNIE." "JUST LIKE OLD
TIMES, ARNIE." "COME ON, ARNIE—CHARGE." *"I
hope he did his sit-ups today,"one lady said. "He does
sit-ups in the morning. It's good for his sore hip."*
They sent him putters and coat racks and wrote him
letters with advice on everything from business to his
hand position in his putting stroke. They fought over

cigarette butts he flipped away, and if he told them to
charge the clubhouse they probably would've.

*By the third round of the Hope Classic, Palmer
looked as if he had a chance. He shot 69 that third day
and was only one shot back of Nicklaus with two
rounds to go. He looked hungry again.*

He'd won all those tournaments, but every time, it
seemed as if he had to prove himself one more time,
maybe to himself, maybe to his father, maybe to those
members back in Latrobe when he was a kid.

*He and Nicklaus both shot 68's that fourth day,
and by Sunday, the NBC people had their drama—
Palmer a shot back of Nicklaus. They were paired
together, and on the first hole, Nicklaus bogied, Arnie
birdied and took the lead.*

*They played almost even through the front nine
and all the way to the sixteenth, where Palmer faced
an eight-footer for a par and Jack had a three-footer
for a birdie that would put him back into the lead.*

Palmer suffered a lot of disappointments during
his career. There were a lot of "almosts." Of the four
most prestigious tournaments, there was one he
never won. The PGA.

Arnie finished second three times in the PGA, but
the most dramatic finish and the closest he ever got
was in 1968 at Pecan Valley in San Antonio, Texas.

Arnie came to eighteen needing a birdie to force a
play-off with Julius Boros. People who heard the
news came running into the clubhouses of their own
golf courses during the middle of their own rounds to
watch the finish on TV. The clubhouse bars all across
America must've been packed that afternoon.

The champion of the people hooked his drive into

the rough. He was a long way from the green and he was in pretty deep rough—there were sticks and broken glass and beer cans and rocks and weeds in there—but he was Arnold Palmer. It was 265 yards to the green, and everybody everywhere watched as he took out a three-wood, backed off, paced, hitched up his pants, then stepped up to the ball. He swung at that ball with everything he had. It came out low and looked like a dub. But then it rose up a little, rose a little higher, higher, drew around a tree, and just about the time it was supposed to die, it got one last lift from everybody everywhere, and carried onto the green. Nobody could believe what they had just seen. All the clubhouse bars all across America were dead still. The TV commentators said nothing. Gene Sarazen, the Hall of Fame golfer, was doing the color, and he finally managed to break the silence, saying simply, "That—just might possibly be—the greatest shot —I have ever seen."

When that gallery at Pecan Valley realized that what they had just seen had actually happened, they began to cheer, louder and louder, and gave a grinning Arnold Palmer a welcome up that eighteenth fairway that might've rivaled the one Hannibal got when he came home from Rome.

Arnold Palmer, greater than great, bigger than life, the God of Golf, was eight feet from the cup.

But Lady Luck isn't much on the upbeat ending. Palmer missed that putt. He finished second.

But the people from Pecan Valley erected a monument on the spot where Palmer hit that shot out of the rough, and it's there today, a plaque commemorating the effort, a monument in memory of what is, what was, and what might've been.

At the Bob Hope Desert Classic, Palmer made the putt on the sixteenth, and Nicklaus missed his. And it all went down to where it's supposed to go for Arnold Palmer—to the very last hole the very last day.

Palmer put his second shot ten feet away. Nicklaus was thirty feet away, downhill. Nicklaus's putt headed for the hole, slowed down and slid. If he made his and Arnie missed, there would be a sudden-death play-off, and Arnie might have another near miss to live with.

But Jack's putt rimmed, and Arnold Palmer, master of drama, stepped up and made his putt. He'd done it again. He flung his visor into the crowd and they fought over it. He was grinning like a little kid, telling the reporters how young he felt, and the look on his face said:

"Arnold Palmer of Latrobe, Pennsylvania, is the new champion!"

6

From a '66 Merc into a 747 Boeing

In his motel room early Monday morning, Rod Curl picked up his copy of the Palm Springs morning paper, tossed every section but the sports into the waste can, and scanned the pages for the column with the results of the Bob Hope Desert Classic. He traced his finger down the column:

Arnold Palmer	71 66 69 68 69	343	$32,000
Jack Nicklaus	64 70 71 68 72	345	14,800
Johnny Miller	70 70 70 63 72	345	14,800
Gay Brewer	66 70 70 68 72	346	7,040
Jim Wiechers	70 69 73 66 68	346	7,040
John Schlee	70 68 69 70 71	348	5,760
Lanny Wadkins	71 70 70 69 69	349	5,120
Kermit Zarley	68 72 70 71 69	350	4,520
John Mahaffey	68 73 68 69 72	350	4,520
Charles Coody	67 75 68 69 72	351	4,000
Billy Casper	68 68 73 71 72	352	3,520
Lee Wykle	71 72 67 69 73	352	3,520
Lee Elder	71 71 72 69 70	353	2,880

Grier Jones	71 69 71 70 72	353	2,880
Allen Miller	70 67 68 75 73	353	2,880
Jerry Heard	71 72 71 71 69	354	2,320
Bob Barbarossa	66 76 70 70 72	354	2,320
Jack Ewing	73 71 69 68 73	354	2,320
Dave Hill	75 70 68 69 72	354	2,320
Mike Morley	71 71 72 71 70	355	1,760
Rod Curl	73 72 68 70 72	355	1,760
Orville Moody	71 68 73 70 73	355	1,760
Lee Trevino	74 70 71 70 71	356	1,380

The $1,760 meant more to Curl than the $32,000 meant to Palmer. That money could be stretched out to four or five weeks' expenses if need be. He'd spent about $2,300 so far, which meant that if he'd missed all the cuts and hadn't made a dime, he would've been back in Redding about two weeks before.

The $1,500 he'd won in the Salad Bowl and the $982 he'd won at the Carlton Oaks weren't official money—they wouldn't count toward the top sixty. But the folks at the United California Bank of Redding couldn't tell the official money from the unofficial.

He had 3,262.25 exemption points, which was short for $3,262.25 official money. He was in seventieth place on the official list, which meant very little right now. It seemed like a long way down the list, and maybe it was, but there was some comfort in knowing that of the ten million golfers in the country, there were only, for purposes of argument, sixty-nine who could beat him.

When he worked on construction in Redding, the only way he figured he'd ever make $1,760 in one week would be in a crap game in Reno or for knocking over a liquor store, which, when the temperature shot up to 115 and the gooey asphalt and pulp-mill stink got to you, didn't seem like a bad idea.

The tour had moved to San Diego. The Andy Wil-

liams–San Diego Open was actually played just outside of San Diego at Torrey Pines, a public course in
La Jolla. La Jolla was a pool lapper's paradise, where
jet-setters and surf bunnies and *nouveau riche* tourists didn't mind paying 20 percent over retail, a kinky
but still unique chunk of the Southern California that
the Beach Boys used to sing about. Most of the 15
percent unemployment was not due to any recession
—it was a matter of pure choice. In La Jolla, there was
legal nude sunbathing on Black's Beach, one could
purchase a bottle of Château Lafite Rothschild for
$325 at a place called the Fancy Pantry, and it wasn't
uncommon to see a surfboard atop a Cadillac Fleet-
wood limo. It was the sort of place that F. Scott Fitz-
gerald would've loved and Ernest Hemingway
would've hated.

And although there was usually a mild breeze off
the ocean and a warm sun, it rained in San Diego
from Monday through Thursday, which hurt the
crowds, but didn't hurt Curl. His 71 that first day was
a good score because of the fact that Torrey Pines was
a long, tough golf course. Curl was what was known
as a good lie player—if he could hit the fairways and
avoid the rough and the fairway bunkers, he could
usually shoot good scores.

The second day the storm left and the crowds
came. Curl's 72 made the cut by three shots, although
because of the perfect conditions it was not a great
round.

Saturday, though, the wind blew hard, and Curl
shot 70, a very good round under those conditions, and
although he didn't have a chance to win, he was in
position for a big check. He was eight shots back of
Bruce Crampton, an Australian who'd had a terrible
time getting people to like him, even on those rare
occasions when he tried. The last day he had a terrible time with his golf game. He shot 76.

Curl battled the windy Torrey Pines course for a 71 that last day, and he knew he was going to make his best check of the year. He and his caddie sat there together talking fast and smoking Tiparillo cigars as they watched the finish and waited to see what kind of money they'd made. Bob Dickson, a tall, bashful-looking fellow, got the $34,000 first prize to take back to the Oklahoma hills where he was born or wherever else he wanted to go.

Curl tied for twelfth place, and he sat down and figured out the payoff. He had just won $3,094, more than twice what he'd started with from Redding. After overtipping everybody, he headed for his motel.

They had enough money now to fly. They found some caddies who would drive their car to Florida, Curl would pay for their gas and oil, and the Curls would fly out Tuesday. The tour was going into the Florida swing, and the Jackie Gleason Inverrary Classic in Fort Lauderdale was the first of four straight tournaments in the sunshine state.

They flew out late Tuesday. The stewardesses had demonstrated the safety instructions for the Boeing 747 so many times that they went through the procedures like robots. Curl was a little nervous about flying, but he felt much comfort in the fact that he was playing the percentages—sitting in the safest section on the safest aircraft in the commercial skies. The 747 was said to be the most aerodynamically sound of all the jets, and he had learned that the back of the aircraft was the safest place in case of a crash. He knew deep down that if one of those things ever went down he would be shooting his pool in the city morgue, but he liked to take every available edge. He had seen so many card games where the man who played the percentages beat the man who was getting the better cards. He'd found much truth to the old saying that the race didn't always go to the swiftest.

He'd told a friend about the statistics on plane crashes and about sitting in the back of the plane, and the friend had laughed at him and said that if your number was up, your number was up. Curl believed that when your number was up, it was indeed up, but he believed that you had two numbers—you got a low number if you were a fool, and a high number if you had good sense.

7

It's Hard to Breathe at High Altitudes

The stewardesses had talked about the oxygen devices that would be used in case of a severe loss in cabin pressure. In a much different way, the air was hard to breathe at high altitudes during a golf tournament too; the higher up you were, and the longer you were up there, the harder it seemed to do a simple thing like draw a breath. Every pro, no matter how good he was, experienced it at some time in his career. And it was something that could never be completely outgrown. *It* was that reaction to pressure, that panic under fire, that momentary self-betrayal that was known as choking.

The Jackie Gleason Inverrary Classic wouldn't be a good tournament for Curl, but it would be a much more traumatic disappointment for Forrest Fezler, even though he would earn over $29,000 for finishing second.

In the middle of a locker-room bull session early that week, a reporter came in looking for Larry Wood.

"He's not here," one of the pros yelled out. "What

you want with Wood? We got Bob Menne, though. You wanna do an interview with Bob Menne? He was the leader in the Robinson."

"For a while," Ralph Johnston laughed.

George Johnson looked at Ralph Johnston. "I would've bet anything my man Ralph wasn't gonna choke it off up there in Hartford."

Ralph laughed. "Got a couple bad breaks. What the hell. It rained. They put trees in front of my ball."

"The Mexican had six shots at Alcan and lost," Jim Dent said.

"Arnold had seven shots at the Open in Olympic with nine holes to go," Menne said.

"Everybody goes through it," Ralph Johnston said. "Arnie, Jack, everybody."

Forrest Fezler was a young polite kid with a solid golf game who looked as if he could've been cast for the part by MGM. He wore the clothes well, and he looked like an athlete, which he was. He wasn't bulky, but he was strong. He played quarterback in high school behind Jim Plunkett, who went on to star in the Rose Bowl and the NFL, while Fezler, wisely, decided to concentrate on his golf game.

Fezler opened up with a 67 at the Gleason Classic. The second day he shot 69, which put him in the lead at 136. The caddies around the practice green late that afternoon were getting out their wallets. One caddie put a $10 bill down on the ground. "Somebody give me three-to-one against Fezler. He's gonna go wire to wire, that young dude."

An older, wiser caddie eased three ten-dollar bills out of his wallet and placed them down on top of the other caddie's ten-dollar bill. "You are *faded,*" he said softly. And then he pointed up at the leaderboard to the name TREVINO, in second place two shots back, and the caddie said, "Fezler's got Lee on his back."

There probably was no human being who knew

more about winning or who played the game with his brains any better than Lee Trevino. He would know about the drainage of the greens; he would know which greens would be hard and which ones would be soft enough to hold a low shot. He knew who was up near the lead and how they would react under pressure. He knew when to make his move and he knew how to make it. He watched the veins in the hands of his opponents for signs of pressure when they putted. He played with a particular plan in mind and he stuck to that plan. And along with the brains and the knowledge, he also had the talent.

Lee Trevino's first win as a pro was the U.S. Open in 1968. He had grown up poor in Dallas (not in El Paso, as many people thought). He had been making $30 a week at a golf course in Dallas and gambled on the side, trying to get his club-pro card so he could go on the tour. When he first played in the 1967 U.S. Open, he was so poor he had to hitch back and forth from his motel to the Baltusrol, New Jersey, country club, and he had to borrow a jacket so he could get into the clubhouse. He won $6,000 for a fifth-place finish in that Open, and $26,472 that year, his first on the tour, and finished in the top sixty.

It seemed at first that Trevino was the greatest thing that could've ever happened to golf. He was a poor kid from the other side of the tracks, and he was a Mexican-American. He would, it was generally hoped, be a champion of the underdog. He was also very funny and talked on and on and on with anyone who would listen. He was a rags-to-riches story, rare in pro golf, and he had a chance to change the very world he'd scrambled out of.

Trevino won four more tournaments between 1968 and 1971, and then in 1971 he won another U.S. Open, a British Open, a Canadian Open and three others.

He was certainly as generous with his money as

most people, but as he became more and more of a
success he acted more and more as if he didn't owe
anybody anything; it was more as if everybody owed
him.

To get a perspective on somebody's character, it's
necessary to see him under adverse conditions. When
Trevino first won, he was in love with the press and
with the world. And then he quit winning. When he'd
shoot a bad round, he wouldn't come into the pressroom, but when he'd shoot a good round, he would
come and remind them about his rags-to-riches career, and they wouldn't be able to get rid of him. He
carried a chip on his shoulder, and he didn't seem to
know how to deal with instant money and instant
fame. One of his early contracts was with *Golf Magazine* as an instructional adviser. Once he got to the
top, he would wait weeks before returning their calls,
if indeed he even did. Perhaps he overextended his
commercial commitments. He knew he had to play
get-it-while-you-can, because if the golf swing went,
he would be back in Texas picking up golf balls at
driving ranges. But there is a certain loss of credibil-
ity when a man comes on hyping everything from
soda pop to aspirin, and it seemed that Trevino
wouldn't breathe if there wasn't a nickel in it.

When he first won, he was the Merry Mex, the
Taco Kid, always a joke, always time for everybody.
He'd gained popularity as a joker, and people expected him to be a joker all the time, even when he
was in a tight spot. His problem was like a night-club
act—when you come out tap-dancing, you'd better be
able to keep the pace.

Palmer and Nicklaus, having been raised around
country clubs, were aware of what they would have
to deal with on the tour, and how they would have to
deal with it.

"You go so long without winning," Trevino had

said, "and you're supposed to be one of the top players in the world—and then you don't win and people start wondering and asking and writing letters and bugging you. Always asking you what the hell's wrong with you, why you're not winning. They expect you to win every goddam week."

"Lee Trevino's changed," one reporter kept saying. "Not the same guy."

Albert Salinas, his road manager, grew up with Trevino. "Lee hasn't changed," he said. "He's the same as he's always been."

Perhaps the public just hadn't got a good look at how Trevino had always been. Or perhaps, to Albert Salinas, Trevino was the same good guy he had always been, and toward Albert he probably was. "Lee's always been a hard worker," Salinas said. "He believes in giving a hundred percent. When he used to work at the golf course in Dallas, he used to pick up all the range balls, drive the tractor, do everything. He didn't have to do all those things, but he figured if he was going to take a man's money, he was going to give the man a hundred percent. And when you have a lot of long-term contracts to fulfill, it puts a pressure on you to keep winning, keep winning."

Every now and then, Trevino would snap at somebody in the crowd. He wasn't having fun like he used to. Sometimes he would say, "I hate this tour. This ain't no kind of life." He wanted to get home and see his kids grow up, he would say. He couldn't handle the lack of privacy the way Arnie and Jack could. Everywhere he went, people recognized him, asked him for autographs, bugged him. But his objections to the pressures and the lack of privacy were sometimes tactless and cruel. After the first round of one 1973 tournament was washed out, Trevino headed in disgust toward the clubhouse when a young kid came up and asked him for his autograph. Trevino shoved the kid, perhaps harder than he'd meant to, and kept going for the clubhouse. In the 1973 Ohio King's Island Open, Trevino was playing in the pro-am, griping all the way around. "I'm not gonna play the last goddam nine holes," he kept saying. "I'm gonna quit. I think I'll just quit." He didn't quit, but he made the amateurs who played with him feel uncomfortable. They had paid good money partly because they were drawn by the prospect of playing with someone like Trevino.

"Some people just can't take the heat. Got a low threshold for pain," someone said.

"It's not easy," one TPD official defended.

A reporter pointed out at a man digging in the heat. "It isn't supposed to be."

In 1974 Trevino won another big one. It was his fifth major championship in eight years. It was the PGA and it left the Masters as the only major championship he hadn't won. In that tournament, he was the Merry Mex again, wisecracking all the way, joking, talking, calling everybody *pardner* and sweet-talking the reporters again. When one of them had asked him if he wasn't a little concerned about not winning in so long, he'd said before the tournament, "Hell, I'm rich, good lookin'—why should I care?" And then he said, "People probably get tired of these jokes. Some of 'em are old. But I suppose if I stop telling jokes, they stop paying to watch me play."

That night at the Gleason Classic, when they went to sleep, both Trevino and Fezler had different kinds of pressures on them.

Everybody waited for Fezler to crack. Inverrary Country Club was a winding 7,128-yard course that had given a lot of good players trouble. Bob Dickson, who'd won the week before, had opened up with a 78.

Fezler was supposed to crack under the pressure that third day. But he made four birdies in a five-hole stretch and shot 68, which gave him a three-shot lead over Trevino. Fezler had never won, and he had a lot on his mind. He was thinking about the $52,000 first prize, the twelve-month exemption, the Masters and the Tournament of Champions, the endorsements and exhibitions, and—very likely—about the man who was three shots behind him.

It was drizzling and overcast on Sunday morning, and Trevino went off ahead of Fezler. On the eighth hole, Trevino stalked his birdie putt, twirled his putter and whistled, stopped whistling, stepped up to the putt and knocked it in. The lead was cut to a stroke.

Fezler had been in the locker room early. He said very little, and when he smiled, he smiled in flashes, almost like muscle twitches. He spoke in quick, short sentences. At this same tournament the year before, Fezler had been denied admission to the clubhouse because a security guard thought he looked too young to be a player. Now he had a chance to win it.

Trevino three-putted the ninth and the lead was back to two. He birdied ten, parred eleven through fourteen, and birdied the fifteenth. Fezler had shot a shaky thirty-nine on the front. But on the eleventh, he hit two big woods and reached the par-five in two and two-putted for a birdie.

Fezler parred all the way to the fifteenth. He looked tense on the tee looking down the last stretch of holes. He had a one-shot lead. He pulled his second shot, a wood shot, far to the left of the 532-yard par-five. He stood over his pitch shot for a long time, and then dumped it into the bunkers between him and the green. He stood there shaking his head. The heat was on, and it was Fezler against Trevino, Fezler against the golf course, and Fezler against himself.

His shot out of the sand was twenty-five feet short of the hole. He missed the putt and bogied the hole.

Trevino, who had finished his round with a 72, came running back to watch Fezler's finish. Fezler stood on the sixteenth tee, his shoulders sagging, pulling nervously at his mustache.

Trevino knew that the stretch holes on the Inverrary course were hard holes, so he had just tried to play them in even-par, knowing that there would be a tremendous amount of pressure that might get to Fezler. And now they were even with three holes to go.

The sixteenth was a 199-yard par-three with a lake guarding the green. It was a choke hole. But Fezler hit a good shot onto the green, and as the crowd cheered, Fezler let out a deep breath.

He two-putted for a par.

Fezler hit the seventeenth green in two and was thirty feet from a birdie which would give him the lead. But he hit the putt weakly and left it five feet short. He stepped up to the putt, stood over it for quite some time, and missed.

He had given the lead to Trevino.

Fezler managed to regain composure on the eighteenth. He put his drive into the middle of the fairway, then decided to hit an easy six-iron to the green 150 yards away. He took a great swing and sent the ball toward the pin. It hit and bit and almost rolled into the hole. A great shot, only four feet from the hole.

The crowds cheered him up the eighteenth fairway. He looked over the putt, then stepped up . . . and missed it.

He had given the tournament to Trevino. He didn't move. He stood there on the green as the reality came over him.

He'd choked.

"What can you say?" he told the reporters. "What's there to say or do when something like this happens?" "It was that second putt on seventeen . . . I just didn't think—I couldn't seem to think clearly. It was hard—

I don't know what . . . I don't really know what happened out there."

Later, Trevino said he had told the kid he felt sorry for him, that he had consoled Fezler and told him not to worry because it happens to everybody.

When Fezler heard that, he said, "He never told me any of those things."

And the next week in Orlando, Fezler decided to be the first one to say something, to let Trevino know that there were no hard feelings, that he could take defeat with grace.

But when he walked up to Trevino and spoke to him, Trevino ignored him, waved at some people he knew and walked away without a word.

8

Are You Running with Me, Rabbit?

Rod Curl had missed the cut at the Gleason Classic, but he was low qualifier for the Florida Citrus in Orlando with a 67. He was hitting the ball dead straight off the tee, but he discovered that he'd been picking his putter up on his backswing. He practiced hard Tuesday and Wednesday on taking the putter back low and slow.

Curl always stayed at the Horne's Motor Lodge in Orlando because they had a special rate, about 20 percent off for the pros and the people connected with the PGA. He was about fifteen minutes from Rio Pinar Country Club. The tournament was sponsored by the Florida Citrus Commission, and there were orange juice stands all over the course. For ten cents the fans could buy an orange and a plastic squeezer.

Curl played early on Thursday and shot 70, which tied him for twenty-fifth place.

On Friday he played late, shot 69, and beat the cut by five shots. He stayed and practiced till dark, then played a few games of pool on the table in the locker room.

One of the pros in the locker room was talking about the true meaning of friendship. At Phoenix, another player who was a good friend of his had picked up a woman in a bar and had taken her back to his room. The woman had been drinking heavily, but she wasn't up to the idea of bringing in a third party. So when he went to get her some cigarettes, he called his buddy on the house phone at their motel. Since they looked so much alike, he told his buddy to get a pack of L&M's and come get the key and go back to the room in his place. He did, took the cigarettes back, climbed into bed, and she never knew the difference.

Curl shot another 69 that next day. Buddy Allin had shot 66–65–67, and his eighteen-under-par total was the lowest of the season. Curl was a long way out of first, but he was in fifteenth place going into that last round. He went to bed early that night, shot his third straight 69, and ended up in an eleventh-place tie.

That finish gave him $3,037.50 for the week, which put him into the top sixty.

Being in the top sixty at this point of the season had no bearing on exemptions—he would have to finish there at the end of the season.

But he was in forty-seventh place with an official $9,393.75, and if figures were facts, there were only forty-six men in the world who could beat him.

He had earned over $6,000 in three weeks, and he was ahead of the rabbit and looking forward to putting some distance between the two of them.

To celebrate, Curl ate prime ribs that night with his wife. He had been able to give his caddie a little extra, and the caddie stopped at a Dairy Freeze. To celebrate, he had them put an extra scoop of ice cream on his banana split.

9

A Hooverville in the Promised Land

On the parkway that leads from Orlando to Miami, a tall black man trotted along the edge of the road carrying two milk bottles filled with water. He was heading toward his '63 Pontiac, parked off the road with the hood up and steam rolling out. The man was a tour caddie who'd been off the tour since the Tucson Open because a hooker had picked his wallet clean the night the tournament ended. He was broke and had to find a janitor's job in Tucson until he saved up enough money to catch back up to the tour, which he was finally doing now.

Back in the 1930's, when the pro tour wasn't worth much, most likely the men who drifted after it to carry the bags weren't worth much either. But after the boom in the 1950's, more and more men, less and less destitute, came out to caddie, hoping to survive the overhead and get lucky enough to get a few winners and see some big money.

The tour was an $8 million Promised Land, but on the outskirts was a tar-paper Hooverville where the caddies existed. They were a ragtag outfit badly fed

and badly led, roustabouts with no last names. Tony
Pro and Angelo and Boogie Tom and Cigar Lou. Toters and Loopers, laughing it up in Hooverville.

Young, old, good, bad, far-wandering, high-rolling
and fast-moving. College boys and drifters, hard
workers and bums. Migrants without crops to pick.

The caddies used to be unofficially run by twenty-
five or thirty old white caddies who weren't too
bright, and race relations were bad. In the 1960's
younger and smarter blacks and whites came out to
caddie and things improved. The caddies are a unit,
but not a union; like most pros, they don't like the idea
of being regimented, and stick together mostly for
protection and survival.

Most caddies are peaceful men, either honest or
not motivated enough to do anybody harm. There are
old men who've found a skill and are experts at reading greens and judging distances and coaching players, and there are old men who would be doing something else if they only could—a notch above
cud-chewing beasts of burden and who run along behind like billy goats and lug the load. There are hustlers and there are hippies who sleep six to a room
and watch the world flash by their mini-bus windows
a week at a time. There are collegians taking some
time off from college, out for a little adventure, amateur golfers who come out to learn the game, welfare
chiselers, no-accounts and interstate skips.

The caddies who work regularly for one player
depend on him for everything from money to protection, and they work agreements to drive the cars
while the players fly. Having a regular caddie is
handy for most players—they find someone they can
trust and someone to run their errands. The caddie
gets the runoff of freebies that the pro gets—shoes
and shirts and slacks that don't fit the pro, and se-
condhand equipment.

The caddies have a hard time at some stops because they are outsiders, because they're black, because they're poor, or because they can't fight back when they're picked on. They usually get treated well in the Midwest and on the West Coast, but they have trouble in the East and parts of the South.

One of the worst stops for the caddies has always been the Doral-Eastern Open in Miami, and this was the week for it, a week the caddies dreaded.

That week, the Doral Hotel and Country Club security people had made sure that the *Codes of Conduct* sheet had been sent to the players to give to the caddies.

The notice was titled "Codes of Conduct for Doral-Eastern Open Tournament Caddies." It said, in part, that "everyone is to remain in their designated work areas," and "under no circumstances can a caddie enter any guest lodge unless he is under the direction and supervision of the contestant. Any disorderly conduct, including fighting, loud or abusive language, loitering, being in unauthorized areas, will result in the revocation of your Tournament privileges and access to the grounds. Wandering throughout the grounds, Clubhouse, and scoreboard area is not permitted."

Even caddies who had never been to the tournament could tell what kind of people they were dealing with—the kind that would put the names of events ("Tournament") and edifices ("Clubhouse") in the upper case, and refer to people ("caddies") in the lower case.

The tournament was to be co-sponsored by the Doral Hotel and Country Club and Eastern Airlines. And down in Miami that week it was business as usual, and as usual, business was hectic. On Miami Beach, an army of old short people walked up and down Collins Avenue. The sun worshipers rubbed on lotion and zinc oxide and turned like meat on bar-beque spits.

The bellhops hustled in the pale ones and hustled out the tanned.

Big jets circled over the ocean and made their approach to Miami International. From the security gate guarding the long driveway at the Doral Hotel and Country Club where the tournament was to be played, the guards could hear the rumble of the big jets when they came in for landings and the whine when they revved to take off.

Outside the hotel, a woman with a blue cast-iron hairdo was wearing her fur coat in the 80-degree heat. The "class" was around the Palm Beach area; the Miami tourists were generally the new rich—people who, given the choice, would rather take a rough ride in a Cadillac than a smooth ride in a Ford. That week, a house organ called *Doral Doings* listed the activities and the goings-on, and told those who couldn't stick around to attend the Doral-Eastern Open, "Just watch for us on nation-wide television—for who knows, you may recognize someone in the crowd other than your favorite pro!!!"

From somewhere, a tough security order had been handed down. It was the height of the burglary season, and there had been a warning to watch the caddies. Some of the guards used this as an excuse to pick on them.

"If it was me," one caddie said, "I wouldn't be watchin' some caddie. I'd figure anybody poor ain't much of a thief. I'd watch the rich guy. If he was a thief, he'd probably be a good one."

The caddies were herded like cattle into a little area where the carts were kept. Like slaves and dogs, they were not allowed to wander around. It was mental torture that they didn't need. After a hard day of work, they weren't allowed to sit down or lie down and rest, and every time they did, they were hassled by the guards.

"We've got a tough security problem," said one of the officials, shrugging. "We got antiques in the hotel. See for yourself. There's a hundred-thousand-dollar chandelier in the ballroom."

A caddie heard that and laughed. He turned to a caddie next to him. "Where we gonna hang it? On our suitcase?"

While the hotel guests sat on the veranda and ate their crabmeat diable en bouche, the security guards were out rounding up caddies.

On Monday evening a black caddie who wouldn't steal the time of day was fishing peacefully at the lake that separated number nine and number eighteen fairways. It was quiet, the sun was going down. A security guard saw that a black man was fishing and that he was wearing a caddie uniform. The guard ran out, took the fish away from the caddie and ran him off the grounds.

On Tuesday a white caddie was drinking a beer and a security man came over, took the beer away and dumped it in a waste barrel and told the caddie he had no business wandering out of his "designated work area." A caddie who was going up to his man's room with his man's clubs was stopped by a security guard. The caddie explained that he had to take the clubs up, and when he talked back to the security guard, the guard had the caddie arrested and taken downtown.

The king of the cowards and the meanest bully on the lot was a guard who had stationed himself between the area where the caddies were and the practice green. Whenever the caddies tried to walk from the caddie area to the green, the guard stopped the caddies and tried to start something with them. He browbeat them, grabbed them and threatened them.

He worked hardest on the black caddies.

White caddies, of course, were harder to spot. When they went into a clubhouse without their uniforms on, they weren't usually asked what they were up to.

"As long as the white college kids keep coming out," said an older black caddie, "things will get a little better for the caddies. They figure we're all niggers, but when they see all the white kids, they scratch their heads and say, 'Hey, hold on here—' And the white kids, they aren't afraid to stand up and talk back."

Most of the players were outraged by the treatment the caddies got. Orville Moody went up to the security guard who was giving his caddie a bad time. His caddie had been around enough not to take that sort of thing. Moody came up to the guard and pointed in his face. "You chickenshit sonofabitch, this man works for me, and if you say one word more, I'll run my fist down your throat. How would you like *that?*"

The security guard knew Orville was serious and he didn't say a word. Finally, Orville left. He saw two caddies sitting down on the grassy bank off the walkway, and he sat down and offered them both cigarettes. "They must figure you guys are all a bunch of criminals," he said. "Well, I'm gonna bust that big security guard if the sonofabitch says another word."

Some of the pros filed complaints about the treatment the caddies were getting. The caddies were part of the show and the pros didn't like the way the Doral people treated them.

Tuesday afternoon a security guard saw two black men talking near the leaderboard. He walked over to them. "You caddies will have to get back there to your players' bags," he said.

One of the black men looked at him. "I might have to caddie *next* week if I don't start doing better ... but as of now, I happen to be playing in the tournament."

The two men were both players, Nate Starks and Pete Brown.

The next day was Wednesday, pro-am day, and the security guards took it easy on the caddies. The officials needed the caddies to work for all of the amateurs playing in the pro-am, so the security wasn't quite as tight.

But on Thursday the caddies weren't needed for the amateurs, and the guards were on them again. "We've got three caddies down here on the bridge," a voice crackled over the walkie-talkie. "Round them up and bring them back to the caddie area," the security man said. A different voice came over his walkie-talkie. "We've got four more down here at the hot dog stand."

Most of the caddies were glad when they finally got out to the course, where they could have some peace of mind.

On Thursday Lee Trevino went out to a four-shot lead with his 64. Rod Curl shot 70 and was tied for ninth. Eastern Airlines stewardesses were being used to drive the players and the press back and forth from the practice tees and the parking lots.

Now that the tournament had started, the security guards, perhaps bored with it all, had eased off on the caddies.

A reporter asked Carroll West if he didn't hate caddying.

"Hate it?" West said. "No. Why should I? It's not always this bad. And anyway, I've got two homes in this world. We get bad names from the drifters, and we can't control their coming in and out. We need a code of ethics. The players are run by a code, so why shouldn't the caddies be run the same way?" West folded his yardage card and put it in his back pocket. "If I come to work dirty, I want somebody to say something about it—*to me.* I can't help but get dirty when I work hard, but I want to look as professional as I can." He slung the bag over his shoulder. "It's not the money. That's between you and the player. But we *have* to have our dignity."

When West left the practice green, he gave a little business pitch to John Jacobs. "J.J., you should've had me last week on your bag. I think I could've kept those seventy-fours off the board for you."

A caddie had to be everything from an errand boy to a parish priest.

In one of the early rounds on Thursday, a rookie wanted to pick up and quit. His caddie took him aside. "Man, you a *pro.* You can *do* it. I know guys out here, they're makin' *fifty, sixty* thousand, can't beat you. You cryin' and all—man, I got all the right yardages, I got all the right pin placements, I can read the greens. All you gotta do is stand there and hit. Let's go on and play the game. That's what you came out here for, wasn't it? To make money?" He reached into the bag and pulled out a six-iron. He slapped the club in the rookie's hand. "This is the club. Hit it."

The rookie hit the six-iron, the ball rose and landed on the front of the green, bounced once and bit about fifteen feet from the hole.

A reporter who'd overheard that exchange said, "You always hear the winner talking about how great he played, how he made the crucial putts, that sort of thing. You hardly ever hear them talk about how their caddies saved it. Just once I'd like to hear the honest truth." He took an imaginary microphone. "Well, folks, I was a goddam basket case out there. I wanted to quit. Didn't have any guts, couldn't read the greens, didn't know what clubs to hit. My caddie did it all. I've got this check for fifty grand, he's down at the bus depot boarding the flyer."

Curl shot 68 the second day and moved into second

place, riding the clouds, just four shots back of Trevino. He stayed up and watched the sports report that night, and when he went to bed he thought about how far down he had been just a few weeks ago.

That night there were the usual traffic jams on the causeways to the beaches and on Collins Avenue. Two Cubans were arrested for holding up a food store, Gonzales and Ecenaro returned $186.60 in the singles perfecta at Miami Jai Alai, and a suspected rapist committed suicide by jumping off a downtown building.

At the Doral Hotel and Country Club on Saturday, the Gazebo Room was packed for the breakfast crowd, and atop the hotel, employees in the solarium were watching the tournament through binoculars.

Curl talked to Alfred Dyer, the black caddie they called Rabbit. "Man," Rabbit complained, "I got enough gas on my stomach to get from here to Charleston." Rabbit Dyer caddied mostly for Gary Player and worked part time for ABC-TV, hauling, setting up and taking down equipment for golf and Monday-night football telecasts. He said he got his nickname because he was a good rebounder in his high school days back in New Orleans.

Rabbit hitched out of New Orleans after high school in the mid-fifties, and went to Los Angeles to caddie in the LA Open. He lucked out by getting Sam Snead for his first bag. He had been on the tour for nearly twenty years, had had more than ten winners, but he hadn't saved much money. But he broke the color line at the British Open as the first black man to caddie in one, and the fans knighted him "Lord Dyer, Sir Alfred of Rabbit."

The Doral Course was one of the hardest courses on the tour. It was 7,028 yards long, and nicknamed, because of the water and the length, the Blue Monster. There were eight big lakes, and the twelfth hole was 608 yards long. Curl would be on TV and he wanted to shoot a nice 65, maybe take the lead, or at least be right up there close. But he was a little tight, he hit too many traps, and he had to fight for his 72 that day. But he was still in the top ten, five shots back of Trevino, who was trying to do it wire-to-wire.

The caddies weren't getting the hard time they'd got during the early part of the week, but one lady in a Doral hat said, "One of them was on marijuana—he had marks all over his arm."

It was of some satisfaction to the caddies that the security guard who'd been picking on them the hardest had been fired after several of the pros complained.

The wind blew hard that last day, but Lee Trevino didn't blow. He shot 71 and won the tournament by one shot over Bruce Crampton and Tom Weiskopf. But four shots back of Trevino was a very elated Rod Curl, who'd closed with a 70 in the wind and tied for fourth. Curl waited to see what he won, and he watched ABC use its short close at the end of the tournament.

Curl immediately called the motel where he was staying and told his wife about his finish. He'd won the biggest check of his career, $6,600, $100 of which would go to his caddie.

Curl was happy because he'd won almost $13,000 in four weeks. The caddies were happy because they were leaving Doral, heading for a new place with new faces and new bars and different places to explore. Some of them hadn't made much money and a few of them were borrowing from anybody who'd lend it. Some of them would have to hitch to Jacksonville for the next tournament.

One caddie was explaining why he couldn't loan out any more money. "I sent my Crosby check to my wife, my Inverrary check to my grandmother, my Citrus check to my girl friend, and I already bet this one on the Boston Celtics."

Six caddies piled into a VW bus and turned a stereo tape-player up full blast as they left the parking lot.

The tour was headed for the last stop in Florida, the caddies moving along it like the men who put up tents in circuses. A ragtag outfit, indeed, badly fed and badly led, roustabouts with no last names. Jabbo and Cricket, Golf Ball and Sissy-Face and One-Arm Bob. Toters, loopers, laughing it up in Hooverville.

Part 2
THE SCRAMBLE

10

The Rumble on the Roof Is Not St. Nick

Every time a circus leaves town, there are people who'd like to leave with it. A lot of waitresses who've overheard the tour talk sigh and go back to eggs-over and the humdrum of soap operas. Clerks in motels will be dropping the names of golfers who've had rooms at their motels. Bus boys and bartenders will stop dreaming, divorcees and secretaries and desk girls and lady scorekeepers who've found exotic romance are now back to their old boy friends and husbands and the security of the local boys, perhaps not realizing that the tour has a boredom and a routine of its own.

On Sunday evening, Bob Wynn packed at his motel and got ready to go to Jacksonville to try to qualify. He saw a friend he hadn't seen in weeks, a rabbit who'd come to watch the finish of the Doral-Eastern before going to Jacksonville.

The rabbit asked him how things were going. Wynn had started the season playing good golf, picking up some good early checks, but now he was doing poorly and he was barely in the top hundred. He was making just enough money to keep going and to prove to his sponsor that he was showing up every week.

"Well," Wynn said, "in plain old shitty English, I'm driving it bad, chipping bad, putting bad and not scoring at all." He tossed his grip into the trunk of his car. "Other than that, and the fact I got up this morning, I guess everything's okay."

All luck aside, there seemed to be those people who could make things happen and those who seemed to always have things happen to them. The security on the pro tour wasn't much better than what it was for dictators in Latin America. Every so often, a tour reporter would be eating a sandwich or having a drink or glancing down the sports page, and he'd scratch his head and say to a friend, "Whatever happened to—" And they would look at their programs and pairing sheets and realize that somebody was either off the tour or down at the bottom. One morning at breakfast, they might notice that somebody wasn't up on the top anymore. They would see some George Archer not even in the top hundred after eleven wins, ten seasons in the top sixty, and over $100,000 for four years and they'd say, "Jesus."

By this time of year, Mac McLendon was thinking seriously about quitting the tour. He'd thought about it several times in the past few years, and now more and more in the past few months.

In six months as a rookie in 1968, he'd won $40,000 and finished thirty-second on the money list. He figured there would be no way he'd miss a $100,000 season in '69. And then he made only the same amount in all of '69 that he'd made in six months the season before. But he'd come close to winning several tournaments in '69, and he figured that if he'd just been long enough to reach the par-fives in two and make those easy birdies, he might've won at least three times.

He became obsessed with distance and tried to change to an upright swing. But he tried to do it without help and he didn't really understand the function of the legs in the swing. He began to swing almost solely with his arms and he messed up the swing he'd had. He picked up so many bad habits that he couldn't get back to his old swing. He'd try one thing that would help temporarily, but it would mess him up even more in the long run. And the rest of his game left him too. His confidence left with it. He dropped out of the top sixty and was a rabbit who couldn't take time off or plan a rest or spend time with his family. He could take it better than his friends and family, however. They didn't know how to react. They were always conscious of what they said and how they said it. When he'd come home after a couple of bad months, they'd say, "Well, you'll win one in the next couple weeks."

But he wasn't even making cuts. He went to a pro back in his hometown of Birmingham to try to get his game back. He'd been willing to make the sacrifices, but in the meantime he hadn't been able to see any daylight and things kept getting worse. The tour used to be fun for him. Practicing, traveling, everything about it that used to be fun was hard work now. The tour was a depressing place now.

If he'd get off to a good start, he'd get too keyed up and start thinking about what he was going to say at the presentation before he'd played six or seven holes. Instead of a good round, he'd lose his concentration and shoot a mediocre round. And then he'd have to struggle to make the cut. Or, he'd have two or three good rounds and choke one round, stick maybe a 76 or 77 in there, and instead of a $5,000 payday, he'd make maybe $500. The little things and the big things all piled up and up, and now, as the tour headed through the Deep South, he was ready to give it all up.

In 1968 Marty Fleckman had already won the NCAA championship and, as an amateur, had nearly won the U.S. Open and the Masters. He was marked for stardom, as they say. He opened his pro career with a victory in the 1967 Cajun Classic.

That was the article Curl had been reading the morning that he went to work out on Interstate 505 near Redding and decided to try to get his tour card. He would've given anything to be in Fleckman's shoes and have Fleckman's life. Now Marty Fleckman wasn't even in the top hundred. He hadn't won a tournament since that first one, and he had scraped up only $2,500 for the season. And now, Curl wouldn't trade any part of his game with the man he used to envy.

In two and a half months, Curl had won more money than he'd won officially in any of his first four seasons. His game had reached a new level, a level of consciousness in golf that could be compared to the levels of consciousness perhaps in music. If he could just keep it going like that for three, maybe four more months he'd get the $40,000 or so that he needed for the top sixty—then he could start hitting for the flags.

Curl left for Jacksonville Monday night feeling good. He was a real success for the first time in his life. However, there had been just a few cards dealt from the deck. There were bad things to come, even signs pointing to them. For one thing, he'd been playing in every tournament without the physical and mental rest that he needed. He knew that he could play only so many weeks in a row and be sharp.

When he missed a few cuts, he was apt to change some little thing and screw up his game the way McLendon had. And then he'd start pressing.

And there were things happening to his life off the course too. His marriage was ending and he knew it. There wasn't much communication between them anymore, and he'd seen it coming for a long time.

He drove and listened to the radio. The Florida stations faded in and out, and he had to keep switching the dial.

The flat Florida swampland picked up enough of the full moon to light the moss hanging off the trees. At a gas station, a tourist from New Hampshire had an overheat and a bad sending-unit in his new car.

Curl's father had been known to place a bet, and Curl knew how fast things could go bad. You always tried to prepare for the disasters when they came. He knew he could hear a rumble on the roof and go to the fireplace, and instead of old St. Nick, it would be ten tons of elephant crap down his chimney.

He tried not to think about it. The sky was clear and the stars came all the way down to the lights from the little houses in the little towns that twinkled in the distance.

11

They Say It Slows Down Your Stroke

There was a TV program called *You Are There,* in which great moments in history were dramatized. The show was believable enough, but had the viewer really been there, he shouldn't have been shocked to hear, even at a great moment, one of the profoundly deep voices say, "Did you see the saddle on that wench?"

So there is no reason to try to exploit the carnal adventures of pro golfers for shock value. Even in ancient times there were probably those young girls who tried to boost their egos by being in the company of the men of the hour. And if they couldn't get Hannibal, his first officer would do.

Like the proverbial mountain, it is there. And the pros who are in the middle of bad marriages, or going crazy, or bored or lonely and find the four walls closing in take advantage of the social opportunities waiting for them at every tournament. If he could qualify for the Colonial Open in Fort Worth, Texas, a hunchbacked cyclops could leave the grounds with a pretty girl.

Young women go in great numbers to the tournaments in Texas, just as they do in Los Angeles, San Diego, Charlotte and Greensboro, Hartford, Atlanta, and all of the Florida stops. But Fort Worth is unique because the women at the tournament are in an unofficial contest to see who can wear the least amount of clothes to the golf course. And the fairways are lined with girls dressed typically in cowboy hats, halter tops and hot pants. Texans don't take their festivals lightly, and the Colonial is a festival, an excuse to party from Wednesday until the last straggler leaves the last party on Sunday.

John Jacobs would go to the Colonial even if the course wasn't suited to his game. Jacobs took over the unofficial reign as the tour bachelor when Doug Sanders remarried. When John Jacobs was fifteen years old, he qualified for the national junior championships in Detroit. And while all the other kids his age were bunked in at the YMCA, dropping water balloons and trying to find a way to cheat the pinball machine, Jacobs checked into a downtown hotel suite, got a fake ID, bought a fifth of Scotch, rented a Cadillac convertible and picked up a twenty-year-old girl. As he neared the age of thirty, he showed no signs of slowing down.

"I used to think that Fort Worth was the best stop on the tour," he said. "But Hawaii's fantastic. You see," he said quite seriously, almost academically, "Hawaii has so many girls on the island. You've got to weigh that. And let's not sell Jacksonville short. Jacksonville, as a matter of fact, is the only place where the girls find out where you're staying and call *you.*"

Jacobs is a powerful man—big in the shoulders, strong in the legs, built more like a tight end than a golfer—with California beach-blond hair and who cuts such a fine figure on parade, he doesn't have to search hard for temptations to yield to. On a vow, he stopped partying for three days at the beginning of one season and finished in a tie for third in the Bing Crosby tournament. A reformed man, fresh with success, he went on to Phoenix. There, he shot a 76 in the first round, allowed two girls to escort him off the course, and several weeks went by before he was seen again on the tour.

Jacobs recalled a dark memory: "They used to play the Robinson Fall Classic in Robinson, Illinois. Robinson is fifty miles from Terre Haute, Indiana, if that tells you anything. It was as bad as Fort Worth is good. They should've never had a tournament there. It was a town of about seven thousand people. And Errol Flynn could not get laid in Robinson, Illinois, with a two-million-dollar bill."

Since the pro is the star of the show, all he has to do when he's on the practice green or if he sees a girl following him on his round—knowing full well she's not there to learn his technique with the middle-irons—is simply to smile at her. If she smiles back, that's it. It's not hard to tell which girls are jock-chasers at the parties they go to. In fact, most of the people who throw the parties along the tour make sure there are stag girls there.

All of the extra-curricular activities are accepted as a part of tour life, accepted even by many of the wives. What is done in a culture becomes in fact what is, if not proper, at least acceptable. And the players who aren't in that sense *players* are conspicuous by their absence.

"You know the girls are nine times out of ten looking for somebody in the limelight at that moment," Jacobs said. "The pros are interchangeable with any other person in the limelight at the moment, but once you know that and once you accept it, you can sure have a lot of fun."

It would be too expensive to be a groupie on the

golf tour, and there aren't many. There are a few girls who travel with a few of the caddies, and there are a lot of girls who come to the same tournaments season after season, or hit three or four tournaments in a close area. There are prostitutes who work a few of the tournaments, especially where there aren't many local girls going to the tournaments, but mostly the hookers make their money off the amateurs who play in the pro-ams or the sponsors who come to tournament stops like Las Vegas.

At every tournament stop, many of the golfers have names from the year before, or they sow seeds for the future, since they'll probably be coming back year after year. "You have to learn to court fast," Jacobs said. "You just have to be frank and lay it on the line. You can save a lot of time and money by being crude sometimes. And there's an old song I heard a long, long time ago. It probably never got too high on the charts, but I always remembered the title." Jacobs paused and poured his beer into his cup. *"I Lost My Baby Because I Courted Too Slow."*

For the wives, it's something they have to learn to live with, or else pack their bags and leave. One tour veteran talked about it. "I never messed around on my wife much before I went on tour. I had maybe one affair. But out on tour it was so easy—I was nearly always gone and my wife was nearly always home. You're in strange towns or at parties and sooner or later, ninety per cent of the guys will."

One of the tour wives said, "I know my husband's going to mess around on me at some time. I can live with it. I just hope the flings are one-nighters. The worst thing would be if he took the girl out to the tournament. That would show disrespect toward me, and I'd lose face with the other wives. You see some players who are married and their wives are your friends, and the players have girls coming in to stay with them for the week—what are you supposed to do? Tell her? I just hope that if my husband runs around on me, he's discreet. Why, you can't sneeze out here without somebody pulling out a handkerchief."

About the most functional relationship for a pro golfer to have is with an airline stewardess, mainly because the stewardesses have a lot of time off and can fly free to the tournaments. The pros meet desk girls at motels, waitresses, lady scorekeepers who walk their rounds with them, and local girls out at the tournaments, but since they fly a lot, they meet a lot of stewardesses. Stewardesses make functional girl friends and good wives. "If you had to be married," Jacobs said, "it might not be so bad to be married to a stew. You could fly free."

As the tournaments end, there are smooth brush-offs and awkward exits, good-riddances and fond farewells. Wives who know and wives who don't. There are local girls dropping names of stars they've "dated," although all there might've been to the date was a bowl of chili at some dive and a quick exit to the room.

And the next week it will be a new town and new adventures. "It's mostly all fun," one married pro said. "It's meant to be harmless. Anyhow, it slows your stroke down, makes you a better putter."

A caddie heard that and shook his head. "You mean, sex makes you a better putter?"

The pro nodded. "The wilder the better."

The caddie was serious. "Damn. John Jacobs ought to be able to make one from here to the end of the world."

12

Too Good
to Last

Rod Curl came to Jacksonville feeling as if the game was getting easy. Everything he was hitting was going straight down the fairway, and almost every putt he hit lipped the cup or went in. It seemed as if there was no way he could keep from making $3,000 every time he played. He shot 70 in the opening round of the Greater Jacksonville Open, then shot 67 the second day and was only one shot out of the lead. He was sure that this would be *the* week.

In the back of his mind, he knew that his golf game would leave him and he would have to find it again. It was that way with almost everybody, even—on a much higher level—somebody like Jack Nicklaus. The difference between most players' problems and Nicklaus' problems was that when they went sour, they missed cuts; when Nicklaus had problems, he'd finish fourth or fifth.

But Curl had not anticipated such an abrupt end to his hot streak. It came on Saturday morning before the first round. As he backed out of a parking place to move his car, a police car banged into the back of him. His Merc was smashed up, and his neck was stiff and sore.

He went ahead and teed off anyway. He shot 77 that day, then shot 75 on Sunday, his neck and back so sore that he had trouble releasing his shots. As it turned out, a 71 and a 70 the last two rounds would've won the tournament. Instead of winning, Curl finished with $800, and he and his family left Jacksonville in a rented car the police department's insurance company had provided. He was in forty-third place with just over $16,000 official.

Curl had made the drive from Jacksonville to New Orleans so many times that he didn't need a road map. There was still a lot of pain in his neck. By Thursday the pain was nearly gone, and he played well enough to make the cut, but then his neck began to bother him again, and he played badly and made only $400.

After New Orleans came Greensboro, and Curl missed the cut. He dropped down to forty-sixth place after Greensboro, almost $80,000 behind the leading money-winner, Lee Trevino, who had already made close to $100,000.

Dave Eichelberger was in sixtieth place leaving Greensboro, with just over $9,000 official, about a dime for every dollar Trevino and Nicklaus had made, and exactly $36.22 ahead of the man in sixty-first place.

Thirty-six dollars and twenty-two cents was just about enough for a bus ticket from Greensboro, North Carolina, to Augusta, Georgia.

13

"And They Can't Swim, Neither"

The Masters tournament in Augusta, Georgia, is private. It isn't connected with the PGA. And more so than any tournament in the world, the Masters is an exclusive affair. It was begun by the great Bobby Jones, who helped design Augusta National's golf course. There is legend, there is lore. And the Masters people even limit the number of spectators allowed to enter the gates, and there are waiting lists just to get on the waiting lists to get tickets to see the tournament. Every year, tickets are scalped for as high as $500 to people who come from all over the world and rent houses for as high as $2,000 for the week.

Rod Curl wasn't playing in the Masters. The only way one could play in such an exclusive tournament was to qualify for an invitation. The Masters, although played on a great and perfectly groomed golf course, was an overrated field of players, mainly because invitations were given to many foreign players and amateurs who, when compared with American tour players, were second-rate.

The foreign players were invited by a Masters committee vote, based on the players' competitive records. In 1975 there were thirteen ways for American players to qualify for a possible invitation:

1. Ex-Masters champions (lifetime invitation)
2. Past five U.S. Open champions
3. Past five British Open champions
4. Past two U.S. Amateur champions
5. Past two British Amateur champions
6. Past five PGA champions
7. 1974 Ryder Cup team (professionals)
8. 1974 World Amateur team (amateurs)
9. Top 24 finishers, including ties, in 1974 Masters
10. Top 16 finishers, including ties, in 1974 U.S. Open
11. Top 8 finishers, including ties, in 1974 PGA
12. Semifinalist in U.S. Amateur
13. Tournament winners of PGA co-sponsored tournaments, designated by PGA as major events, from one Masters to the next

Those were the general guidelines set by the Masters committee, but qualifying for an invitation didn't mean that a player would necessarily get one. It was almost academic that he would, but technically the Masters committee could invite or exclude anyone on that list.

In 1959 Charles Sifford, the only black player on the tour at the time, went into the last round at the U.S. Open at Winged Foot Golf Club in New York knowing that a good finish could win him a place among the top sixteen finishers and qualify him for a possible invitation to play in the Masters.

A reporter from Augusta took note of Sifford's chances and said, "If that nigger finishes sixteenth, we may just take the top fifteen; if he finishes tenth, we'll just take the top nine; and if he finishes second

. . . then we'll just take the winner."

A black had never played in a Masters tournament at that time. Golf was a white man's game, and the Masters was a white social affair at a white man's sanctuary. Outside the Augusta National gates, poor whites and blacks hand-farm the outskirts. You might walk into a bar and hear a nasal country voice singing about hard luck and unrequited love, but inside the gates of Augusta National, you will find no Fort Gordon noncoms telling off-color jokes over crushed cans of Jax beer. Most of the members at Augusta National have never seen the inside of a bowling alley or the top of a ditch from the bottom, and could look upon a fifty-year-old black caddie and say, "Hey, boy."

Every year, black people were invited to participate in the tournament—to carry bags, to serve food, to shine shoes. And downtown in Augusta, the inscription on the Confederate monument reads, "No Nation Rose So White and Fair . . ."

The history of the black golfer on the pro tour isn't as tragic as, say, the history of the black man in Tallahatchie County, Mississippi, but it isn't glorious, either. Since golf had been a rich man's game, there naturally weren't many black men playing it. The same bigots who could point with arrogance to the fact that black men weren't good swimmers (forgetting the fact that they weren't allowed on beaches and in pools) could point to golf and say that they weren't good golfers either.

The first black player to pioneer the tour was Teddy Rhodes, a gifted golfer whose talents had faded by the time he was allowed to tee off in major competition. He was allowed to play in USGA (United States Golf Association) tournaments, one of which was the U.S. Open, which he nearly won, but he wasn't allowed to compete in PGA events. There was a clause in the PGA bylaws which stood until 1962. It was Article I, Section III, of the PGA Constitution, and it specified: "For professionals of the Caucasian race."

After Rhodes came Charlie Sifford. Sifford was a very talented player whose trademark cigar seemed to be eternally short, perhaps because he got so many doors slammed in his face. Sifford was thirty when he started opening the doors of the PGA tour in 1954. He was the only black player on the tour at the time, and at the tournaments he was able to play in, most of the fans looked at him as if he had a tail.

Since the "whites only" clause was still in effect, Sifford wasn't actually a PGA member and didn't have to be allowed to play in tournaments. Some of the tournaments in the North allowed him to play, but he was barred from the tournaments in the South, and that meant that he would have to let his game go sour while the tour swung through Dixie. He had to go it alone during the fifties, and he often had a hard time just finding a motel near the course which wouldn't turn him away. He suffered a lot of abuse, and had he been able to concentrate on shot-making, had he not been barred from so many tournaments, he might well have been one of the stars of the era. Sifford was playing in the Greater Greensboro Open one year at a time when finishing in the top sixteen there qualified a player for the Masters, and it looked as if he had it cinched. And then he went to one hole on the back side, and a crew of drunken rednecks was waiting for him. They started yelling "Nigger" and whistling and hooting on his backswing. They followed him down the stretch and threw things at him. It was all Charlie Sifford could do just to finish—out of, of course, the top sixteen.

In 1963, at the age of twenty-eight, Pete Brown became the second black tour-regular. Brown had won the UGA championship (United Golf Association) at the age of twenty, in 1955. The UGA was primarily a black tour, known to most black players as "the chittlin' circuit." Brown had grown up around Jackson, Mississippi, and after he won the UGA a man came to him and asked him if he'd like to live in Detroit. Two weeks after he moved to Detroit, Brown got infectious mononucleosis and was supposed to die. "It's a good thing I went to Detroit," he said later. "If I'd been in Mississippi, I would've died in the hallway." In Detroit, there wasn't the kind of discrimination in the hospitals that there was in Mississippi, and Brown got the best treatment from doctors who at one point gave up on him. But he didn't die. Even then, he was supposed to become paralyzed and blind. But he kicked the paralysis, opened his eyes, and was able to play golf again. The man who'd brought Brown to Detroit sent him to California and backed him in a few PGA tournaments in which he was allowed to play. But the backer died shortly after, and Pete Brown went back to Jackson, Mississippi, and back to the "chittlin' circuit." "If you could call it a circuit," he said. "Sometimes they didn't have prize money, and sometimes there wouldn't be a tournament for months."

Brown went on the PGA tour after winning the 1961 and 1962 Negro National Opens. The "white only" clause had been struck down, but even then Brown and Sifford weren't automatically allowed to play in tournaments. The tournament committees would make them play special qualifying rounds, and if they made it through they still weren't obligated to let them play. "You had to promise," Brown said, "that you wouldn't use the locker room or try to eat in the dining room or even enter the clubhouse for any reason. You'd play your round and be gone."

In 1964 Pete Brown became the first black man to

win a major PGA event, the now defunct Waco-Turner Open in Oklahoma.

"I was worried down there in Oklahoma," he said. "But it was ten times worse up North in Columbus, Ohio, the next week." They were playing the PGA championship, which Brown had qualified for with his win at the Waco-Turner, and the folks at the host Columbus Country Club had never had a black person in their clubhouse except to serve food. No black person had ever used the locker room. He had things thrown at him, he got called all kinds of names, and his life was threatened.

Brown wasn't invited to the Masters, however. At that time, winners of a PGA co-sponsored event weren't automatically invited. But at that time, and for years after, past Masters champions were given a vote on whom to invite. They could've easily invited Brown and Sifford, who were two of the better players on the tour at that time. But the past champions ignored the issue.

In 1964 the players took control of their own organization, splitting from the PGA and the rule of the club pros, forming the Tournament Players Division of the PGA, which governs the tour today. They elected their own commissioner, Joe Dey, a former golf writer, historian and chairman of the USGA. The players were issued players' cards, and Brown and Sifford were official members. And by this time, with civil rights for blacks a national issue, the Masters in Augusta became a symbol of racial prejudice. But if the new TPD put any pressure on the Masters people to invite a black player, it wasn't public pressure.

In 1967 Charlie Sifford won the Greater Hartford Open. In 1969 he won the LA Open. In 1970 Pete Brown won the Andy Williams–San Diego Open and lost two others in play-offs. And by this time the racial issue had tainted the gloss of the Masters to such a degree that the Masters people wanted to get it over with and invite a black player.

By this time there were other blacks who'd come onto the tour after most of the hostility had been softened by what Sifford and Brown had swallowed. And by this time, Sifford had passed fifty and Brown neared forty. So each time a black player came onto the scene, he was examined under what must have seemed like a giant microscope. Would he be the first black superstar? Would he be the man to break the barrier at the Masters? Would it be George Johnson, a former Columbus, Georgia, star athlete? Would it be Rafe Botts, the one-time caddie? Would it be Charlie Owens with the cross-handed grip? Would it be Charlie Sifford's nephew Curtis, or Chuck Thorpe with all that talent, or little Nate Starks or big Jim Dent who could hit his one-iron as far as Nicklaus could hit his driver? Or would it be Lee Elder?

Elder was born in Texas and used to hustle golf, which was the only way he could make money with his game. At one point in his career, he hooked up with the legendary hustler Titanic Thompson, toting Titanic's bag. They would go to some course where suckers sometimes pulled up in taxicabs with paper sacks full of money.

Titanic was in charge of the haircut, Elder was in charge of the shave. When Titanic beat the right mark, he'd stick the needle in. "Why, I bet you couldn't beat that old nigger caddie of mine," he'd say. The man would grab the bait and Elder would beat him flat.

Later, Elder would give his opponents all sorts of handicaps—he'd drive with a pop bottle, wear overshoes and heavy coats, or tie one hand behind his back.

Then Elder played the chittlin' circuit. The prize money was small, but there were enough $500 and

$1,200 first prizes that Elder could make a living. At one stretch, he won twenty-one of twenty-three events.

By the time he and his wife Rose scraped enough money together for the tour, he was thirty-four years old. In his rookie year of 1968 he won $31,691, but more significantly, he tied Jack Nicklaus and Frank Beard in the American Golf Classic on national television. In sudden-death, it came down to Elder and Nicklaus, and Elder took him to the fifth hole before Jack finally won the play-off with a birdie. He won $53,000 in 1969, had an off-year in 1970, then came back with $50,000 in 1971.

In 1971, with public opinion mounting critically against them, the Masters people amended their rules. Anyone who won a major PGA tour event would automatically qualify for an invitation to the Masters. The rule wasn't retroactive, however, and Charlie Sifford and Pete Brown couldn't qualify on past per-formances. And the black players, as well, didn't want to enter Augusta National through any back doors.

From 1971 on, the subject of a black man in the Masters was done to death. Every time a black player was leading a tournament or was in contention, the question would be fired at him about the Masters— not "How's this course playing?" but "What about that Masters?" There was enough to worry about without having the Masters on their minds, and it got so the black players hated to hear anything about the subject. They often refused to talk about it, or else they came to hate it.

The Masters people were privately hoping that Dent would be the first black to play in their tourna-ment, since at one time he had been a caddie at Augusta National.

But Dent, too, was sick of the subject. "You can't

live on that Masters money," he would say. "If I win a tournament, well, that'll be *my* Masters."

But Elder still wanted to play in the Masters. He wanted it very badly. He kept scratching at the door but he couldn't get it open. In 1973 he finished in a tie for second in the USI Classic in Sutton, Massachusetts. Although he shot 64–69–69–67 at the Sammy Davis–Hartford Open, he lost in the first hole of a sudden-death play-off to Lee Trevino. He finished fourth at the Colonial, fifth at the Crosby, sixth at New Orleans, seventh at Greensboro, seventh at Atlanta and tenth at the Monsanto in Pensacola. He began to believe that he'd never make it.

And then the press began looking to Dent as the Great Black Hope.

But in April of 1974 Elder went to Pensacola for the Monsanto, played at a golf course which had barred black players from its clubhouse just a few years before. He went into the last round two shots behind the leader, Peter Oosterhuis of England. Oosterhuis parred seventeen and faced a two-foot putt on eighteen that would kill Elder's chances. But Oosterhuis blew the putt.

The black Texan and the Englishman went into a play-off, the third play-off of Elder's career. On the first three sudden-death holes, Oosterhuis twice had short putts that would've ended it—but he missed them both.

Elder had an eighteen-foot putt on the fourth sudden-death hole that would give him a victory. He sank the putt and the crowd went wild, gave him a sustained, emotional ovation, and Elder cried.

Elder would be the first black man to play in the Masters.

It was over, and the black players and the Masters people were relieved.

Clifford Roberts, the man who runs things at the

Masters, met Elder for the first time at the New York Metropolitan Golf Writers dinner prior to the U.S. Open. The two stood up and shook hands and the crowd stood and applauded. They were not necessarily applauding either man but, rather, expressing their delight that things had changed for the better.

And it was very ironic. Because of the national impact of Elder breaking the barrier at the Masters, Elder would become a rich man. Perhaps poetic justice. Because had Elder been white, the Monsanto win would've meant very little compared with the meaning that win took on. The Masters had been a menace to Elder and the other blacks, but now it would be a gold mine to him. He became an instant national heroic symbol, written up in nearly all of the magazines, and invited to play golf with the President of the United States.

Elder's phone rang almost continously for weeks.

He would never again have to play with one hand behind his back.

The racial prejudice on the tour had been diminishing—at least among the players—long before Elder broke the Masters barrier. "When I first came on the tour," Mac McLendon said, "I had a very bigoted viewpoint. I grew up in Alabama and went to school at LSU, and there were certain things you grew up believing that weren't true. But when I got to traveling the tour and got to know the black players I realized how wrong I had been."

But as mentioned before, the black players are still mistaken for caddies at some of the tournaments, since most caddies are black and there are so few black players. The black players understand it, but they get tired of having to prove they're players week after week. Pete Brown still plays the tour, and he told one of the TPD officials that he ought to post the pictures of the black players at the gates every week. "You could just come in and tell the guard, 'Look, I'm that one up there,' and go on in."

The biggest problem for black players today is not racial prejudice, but finding backers. One might guess there would be a lot of limousine liberals dying to back black golfers. But there aren't. Backing a golfer is a risky business in the first place, and there aren't many black businessmen interested enough in golf to sink their money into backing some unproven player.

The black players have few contracts and endorsements, since they haven't exactly shaken the world yet. George Johnson, perhaps the finest dresser on the tour, has no clothing contract. Pete Brown has a clothing contract, and was a member of the Haig Ultra staff until Haig decided to stop paying pros to play their equipment. And Dent has begun to capitalize on his long-distance hitting.

But because of the Masters, Elder got bombarded with endorsement offers. Elder was so busy with finance that he had to neglect his golf game, and he was playing poorly by the time his shot at the Masters finally came.

Augusta, as it always does, came to life for one week in April, a drowsy town that raises its shades one week a year and then goes back to sleep.

Even the churches get in on the act. One year, one of the Augusta Baptist churches put on its Sunday marquee during Masters week: WHEN CHRIST AROSE, GOD PLACED THE MASTERS JACKET ON HIM.

Green sport jackets are brought in from New York, Masters insignia are sewed on, and the jackets are sold for about $30 more than people could've bought them for without the 99-cent insignia. There are overpriced Masters hats, shirts, socks. Hanging Masters baskets, "Mastersburgers" at a truck stop, WELCOME

MASTERS banners on everything from the Piggly Wiggly store to the rollerways and gas stations: *Lost Wilderness Gas Station—Oil Filters changed, Lube Jobs*—WELCOME MASTERS. In one yard where there were chickens flapping and three rusted cars jacked up on blocks the owner had sprayed one car with green paint that read WELCOME MASTERS.

More than half of the population of Augusta is black. All of the caddies at the Masters have been black. Under the rules, only Augusta National caddies are allowed to work the Masters. The fact that all Augusta National caddies are black prompted one of the black-readership newspapers in Augusta to ask—since the city wouldn't think of having all black policemen or firemen or teachers—why it insisted on having all black caddies at the Masters.

Those were things that still existed, and just because Lee Elder had been invited to play in the Masters golf tournament, it didn't mean that people had buried all of their prejudices. But someday there will be a black superstar in professional golf, someone with the ability and the draw of a Palmer, a Nicklaus or a Trevino. Black kids will start playing the game, and there will be enough black players on the tour that their pictures won't have to be posted at the gates.

Lee Elder missed the cut in that Masters. There were no incidents. Everything was rather smooth and pleasant, despite a few rednecks who cheered and clapped when he missed a putt. Teddy Rhodes, Charlie Sifford and Pete Brown weren't there physically, but they were there in spirit, and Lee Elder, although he didn't win the tournament, had accomplished something more important—he had taken down the last WHITE ONLY sign in golf, and removed a psychological barrier to success.

14

The End of Something

Rod Curl had begun a deep dip and a long slide. In four weeks he had gone from thirty-first to forty-third. The week after the Masters, he played in Pensacola at the Monsanto and missed the cut and dropped to forty-sixth. The next week, they played the Tallahassee Open, and he thought he'd got it going again. He made $1,000. The week after that, the tour went to Dallas for the Byron Nelson Classic, and he made $1,500. But he had been lucky to score as well as did, he was hitting the ball so poorly. And the next week at Houston he missed the cut and dropped back down to forty-eighth. He was trying little changes in his swing, which not only wasn't helping, but was taking him farther away from that groove he'd found in March.

He made $243.50 at the Colonial and dropped down to fifty-second place, and when the tour came to Memphis it was the middle of May, he had no momentum, a bad attitude, a stiff neck and a shaky marriage.

Rod and Bonnie Curl had been high school sweethearts and were married right after graduation. Rod had a lot of respect for Bonnie. She was a good woman. When he first quit his day job and decided he wanted to be a pro golfer, she had gone out and got a job so he could do it. But they'd married so young, and as they found out, sometimes people drift apart after they grow up. Curl didn't want to be a bachelor—he liked having a wife on the tour, but it just didn't seem like there was enough there to hold things together.

It was hard to hold a marriage together on the tour, but it was hard to be on it without one. A tour wife is lover, suitcase packer, mother, secretary, companion, bookkeeper, travel agent, accountant, tax consultant, relief driver, cheerleader, ball shagger, psychoanalyst and friend.

In the locker room at the Danny Thomas Memphis Classic, Bob Wynn talked about his wife. "I don't know how I ever made it on my own. Maybe I didn't. She's the thinker. She sees an old man walking along, she wonders who he is, if he's happy, does he have a family, does anybody care about him. Me, I just say, 'Well, there goes another old man.' "

Over on the other side of the locker room, Tom Watson was looking through his mail.

Even before Linda Watson married Tom, she knew a lot about life on the tour. She had met Tom Watson while doing a play in high school in Kansas City. Most of Tom's life was already golf. He won the Missouri State Amateur championship four times while they were going together. While they were engaged, he went on tour in 1972 and Linda worked at her father's real estate firm in Kansas City.

"I wanted him to see what the tour was like and what life was like on the tour without a wife. I wanted him to have his good times and his flings and whatever he wanted to do. I was hesitant about marrying a golf pro and the kind of life he'd have to offer me. I tried to be very realistic about it, because I'd watched Tom come home from the tour and he would be sick or tired or worn out from the grind. I knew it would be a harder life than what I'd expected. But I did expect it to be glamorous to a certain extent. Like the big formals that would come up after the pro-ams. I thought, *Oh, great, go get 'em.* I thought that you'd go in and just have a great time at the parties all week. And I brought all my long formals when we first got married. But I found out I couldn't take it. The amateurs go out and it's one week out of a year for them. They've been looking forward to this all year. If you're a top-forty money-winner, you have this every week playing in a pro-am. You can't always take all the parties, because you have early tee-times the next morning. The amateurs want to stay up late, and who can blame them? But the bands and dinners get to be a routine that you can't take week after week. So you leave the formals at home."

Tom Watson won over $70,000 in 1973, the year he and Linda were married, so she didn't have to suffer with a pro who wasn't making it on the tour.

"I tried for a while to have things exactly right and to think of the right things to say if Tom was coming back to the motel after a disappointing round. And then I realized, Hey, we're married, we have a life to share together. I can't one hundred percent cater to my husband. Maybe that's something wrong that I'm doing, I don't know. But I feel we have a life to share, where he's supposed to share and please *me* the same as I'm supposed to share and please *him.* I try to do everything I can to please him. But he has to pull himself up partly on his own."

Tom Watson perhaps doesn't have the problem of keeping his spirits up the way some players do, because in 1974, his third year on the tour, at the age of twenty-five he won $135,000. And his wife was always there to cheer him on during every round. Because they had no children, she could walk the courses. She liked to walk the courses. Some wives prefer to be pool sitters and lobby sitters or clubhouse socializers. And the women with small children usually have to stay back at the motels.

The friendships that form among the tour wives usually depend on what types of wives they are— walkers are friends with walkers, pool sitters become friends with pool sitters. But the friendships were based, first of all, on whether the husbands got along with one another. Before the big money came, there were more cliques and there was more socializing. The families were closer knit and always ate together, drank together and partied together. They stayed at the same motels. In those days nearly all the pros and wives made it to pro-am parties and lived it up when they could. The pros then were making a decent living on the tour, but that was about it. Most of them were in it mainly for the good time they could have. But even today, the tour is like a small town, like a little Peyton Place. Everybody knows who everybody else is, and as in any small town, there's strain between the old friends of some player's ex-wife and his new wife.

"There's a certain kind of woman," one of the wives said, "who ruins a husband-and-wife relationship and then he ends up marrying her. A lot of people get very upset and unhappy about it."

Some tournaments have good baby-sitting facilities, so the wives get a chance to shop or get out to the course. The week of the Memphis Classic, Leslie Thompson, Leonard Thompson's wife, was out to the tournament. She rarely goes to the course to watch her husband. "If he had a job as an accountant, I wouldn't go down to watch him work. And anyway, if I'm out there, I know that Leonard's concerned about me moving when somebody else putts or hits a shot, and that's just one more thing that he doesn't need on his mind. And when it's over, we don't talk about golf. There are a lot of other things to life than business, so Leonard tries to leave it at the course."

And while the players are out at the courses the wives who don't go out to watch are sometimes provided with outings and luncheons. Preston Trail, where the Byron Nelson Classic is played, is an all-male club and there are no facilities for women. Most of the women realize that they're not part of the show and they don't mind the fact that they're not allowed in the clubhouse, especially since the tournament provides a very nice trailer, plenty of food, and baby-sitting service practically around the clock.

Tom Watson's situation was somewhat like Curl's in that he sometimes didn't see his old friends.

"Tom's first year on the tour, he had to qualify," Linda Watson said. "And after that, he was exempt. So we never saw too much of the friends we had made that first season. There are a few wives, of course, who play the social-status game—when your husband becomes exempt or wins a tournament, they'll come up and suddenly acknowledge the fact that you're alive. They'll be talking to you—whereas before, they wouldn't—and asking you to go places with them.

"Jack Nicklaus' wife is probably the nicest of all of the wives. Barbara Nicklaus has six children, but she gets to quite a few of the tournaments. She's warm and friendly and never forgets a name or a face. And she makes you feel important."

Arnold Palmer's wife, Winnie, lived in a trailer and traveled the tour with Arnie when they were first married. Now that they have two grown daughters, she goes to just a few tournaments, and keeps a low profile when she does.

Not many wives travel in trailers anymore, but they spend a lot of time in hotels and motels, and some wives make up lists of the best hotels and motels in different tour towns. They rate them as they travel, and give the lists to the other wives, making note of which ones have hard beds, which ones are clean, where the service is good—updating Duncan Hines. Other wives keep lists of restaurants, shops, shopping centers and laundromats.

"Lou and Patsy Graham's daughters are nearly grown," Linda Watson said, "and she can go to a lot of tournaments. Patsy has more fun than anybody. She's always going and she knows every town. She can take you on a complete tour of Washington, D.C., and she never goes to New York without going to at least one matinée of a play during the week. She knows every shop and every show and if you go to a foreign country, and if you're with Patsy Graham, then you're going to see *everything.*"

Some tournaments try to help the wives see everything. But the best tournaments for the wives are probably Disney World and King's Island in Cincinnati. Disney gives the wives passes to the theme park and has a family fun night for the players and their families, and King's Island gives the wives unlimited passes into their amusement park.

But it isn't all fun. While the players get their yardages on Mondays and Tuesdays, the wives scout out the restaurants and laundromats and shopping centers. They do the laundry, usually in pairs, because it's safer that way. They might go back to the motels and check airline schedules for Friday afternoon if they miss the cut or Sunday or Monday if they make it. Or get out the log books and write down the mileage if they're traveling by car, or what the rental cars and meals and rooms and dry cleaning and laundry and entertainment have cost them the week before. Or make up lists of what has to be done next week, where the Monday charity pro-ams are if they're lucky enough to be invited to any, and where the exhibitions are, if they're lucky enough to get them. Or head for the shopping center or go out to the pro-ams and visit with the amateur partners after the round, giving the husband a little relief. Or spend time with the other wives going to movies and museums or sightseeing, or going to luncheons or helping out by entertaining some business person who has come in to deal with her husband, chatting with him in the clubhouse while her husband finishes his round.

"I guess," Linda Watson said, "that most people think that tour life is nothing but glamour. There are a few wives that the people at the tournaments look upon as celebrities too—the Johnny Millers, the Nicklauses, the Trevinos and the like. And there are probably some people who get spoiled by the treatment. But I think a lot of the attention isn't so much to pamper you as it is to help you out. We have a hard time in that we don't know the cities, the restaurants, the streets. And sometimes we're without a car. If it wasn't for the help the tournament people give us, we could end up in the worst parts of town."

Being on the road has its disadvantages, but there are good things about that kind of life. "We have friends who've moved around the country and we might not get to see them more than every five years if we lived in different towns," Linda Watson said. "But we get to see them three times a year in some cases, and we can redevelop our friendships every year. That keeps you up."

The wives try to keep their husbands' spirits up after bad rounds. Winnie Palmer once told Arnie after a bad putting round that he was moving his head. He thought about it, realized she was right, and after correcting it, he went out and won the tournament.

One of the first times Tom Watson was leading a tournament, Linda came back to the condominium where they were staying. "I went to the room," she said, "and I started complaining about *everything*. I started crying and I had my hands up in the air and I was pointing at everything, and finally Tommy put his arms around me and said, 'Honey, you're choking.' And he was right. After he lost the tournament —well, we'd never had to deal with that. I didn't know exactly what to do. He came into the kitchen and I just said, 'I guess we blew it.' And he said, 'I guess so.'"

Rod and Bonnie Curl had been putting their divorce off for a long time. The children, the money problems, Rod's career—those were all excuses to avoid hard realities. But at Memphis, they finally faced it. They talked it out and it wasn't pleasant, but they managed to discuss rather than argue. And after a long talk, they decided that it was over. They would get a divorce. There wasn't a lot of bitterness. Modern society and the pressures of the tour had had a lot to do with it. But they both agreed that what was over was over. They vowed not to use the kids as a weapon to get back at each other. They'd try to be good parents, they'd try to remain friends, and they'd try to remember the good times.

They split the proverbial sheets, and Bonnie and the children headed back to Redding. Rod drove them to the airport and watched the plane take off. He felt a sort of guilt, a sense of relief and a strange feeling of confusion.

It was the end of something, and he didn't altogether like it. He drove back to the golf course, alone.

15

It's Only a Game?

Curl had too much on his mind to concentrate on golf. He had trouble sleeping, and he didn't seem to have any energy. He missed the cut at Memphis, and again the next week at Atlanta. He didn't qualify at Charlotte, and as the tour made its first swing north, he had slid to fifty-sixth place and was back out there on Mondays. And going into the month of June, his game was as messed up as his mind.

He qualified for the Philadelphia Classic, but he missed the cut again. When this sort of thing happened when he was a rookie, he would wonder whether he'd lost it for good. He knew now, however, that his game would come back, but he didn't know how or when. He was getting edgy. He had less patience with his caddie, with waitresses, with operators on the phone. He wasn't allowed to throw clubs, but he wanted to. Under the TPD rules, he *was* allowed to bury a clubhead in the ground. He was hitting the ball so badly that he had to find some way to get it out of his system. So he found creative ways to bury clubheads in the earth. He made games out of it. He buried them backhanded and forehanded and worked on his side-arm.

As he went through these times, it was a lot easier to understand somebody like Dave Hill.

Hill had been tagged as a sort of rebel, a hothead, which was probably the only side of the man that the public, through the press, ever really saw. Hill was a perfectionist and, in Curl's opinion, one of the best shot-makers ever. There seemed to be no weaknesses in his game, and Curl often wondered how this man ever shot over par. Hill was, however, sometimes his own worst enemy, and his temper could get the best of him.

Dave Hill was five-one and weighed a hundred pounds when he graduated from high school. "I was in fights all the time," he said. He'd stuttered through grammar school, and his temper was probably what helped in his survival. Hill grew up on a farm in Michigan on the edge of the Jackson Country Club, and he and his brothers caddied. Even when Hill was five-one, he was a good player, and he went to work at a country club after he got out of high school. And then he grew to be five-eleven, and he went on the tour. IIis first few years were tough. He was married and had a child and there wasn't much money coming in. He won two tournaments when he was twenty-three, another tournament two years later, then developed a very small problem with his grip.

"You wouldn't think a little thing like that could cause so much trouble, but it did. I tried everything, and I lost my confidence. It lasted for three or four years, until Ben Hogan and Manny de la Torre finally straightened me out. Even for a long time after that, it was hard to get my confidence back."

It was during that time that he started getting fined a lot. "Oh, hell. I've been fined so many times, I quit keeping track." He said, "You grind it out week after week, month after month, and you get to the end of the tunnel and there's no light. You have to keep playing even when you're playing awful, and things that don't normally bother you start to eat you alive. The pressure builds and pretty soon it's like a boiler. The littlest thing's going to set it off. When you hit a bad shot, the only thing you can do is throw a club or break one or cuss. You've got to get it out of your system before you get to your next shot. I cuss pretty hard when I hit a bad shot. Not real loud. I tell the lady scorekeepers that if they can hear me cuss, they're standing too close. They've got to realize they're not at a church social."

Hill's ex-caddie, Junior Moore, likes to tell the stories about Hill's fines and suspensions. "We did some wild things. I remember one time he was so mad that he said, 'Junior, I wish to hell I had a machine gun. I'd mow the whole gallery down.' Then we laughed and started to cut up and it didn't bother him any more."

In 1967 he finally won the Memphis Open and made it back to the top. The press loved Hill because he was never one to hold back his feelings or opinions.

"Hell," he said, "if a newspaperman asks you a question, even if it's loaded, you ought to give him an honest answer. If he asks you how the course was and you say it was great, and he knows there was crabgrass on the greens and no grass on the fairways, he's gonna think you're smoking something funny."

The most publicized Dave Hill incident was at the 1970 U.S. Open in Chaska, Minnesota, when he criticized the golf course, made sports headlines, had the galleries down on him and, of course, got fined.

"It started out as a damn joke, and people took it serious. This is one reason I don't trust the press. I'd flown into Minneapolis and the girl at the motel told me we were right near the course. Well, the next day it was a two-hour cab ride before we located it. I'd been playing a practice round with Palmer, and he and a lot of others had been griping about the condition of the course, so when I got to the pressroom, the first question right out of the box was, 'How did you find the golf course?'

"And I couldn't resist. I said, 'Hell, I'm still lookin' for it.' And everybody laughed. Somebody asked what the course lacked and I said, 'Forty acres of corn and a few cows. Somebody ruined a good farm when they built this course.' "

One joke led to another and everybody was laughing. But when it came out in the paper the next day, the story had lost the humor. So Hill decided to play the devil's advocate. "This is a rotten course," he told the reporters, "but I'm gonna win the tournament anyway." And he nearly did win. By the last two days, he'd won the galleries over, and he finished second to Tony Jacklin.

He'd finished second on the tour with $156,000 in 1969 and won the Vardon Trophy for the lowest scoring average on the tour. He won three tournaments that year and made the Ryder Cup team, and then, after 1970, he began to cut back his schedule of play.

But the reporters played up the Hill temperament as often as they could. At St. Louis in 1973, there was a story that Dave Hill flew in, took one look at the course, checked out of his hotel and withdrew from the tournament. "I not only wasn't entered in the tournament, I've never even been to St. Louis except to change planes."

Earlier that same year, Hill had been at the Doral–Eastern Open and was invited to the pressroom. The reporters were talking to Lee Trevino, and when Trevino got up to leave, the reporters left with him, leaving an angry Hill there alone, except for four reporters who stayed.

The next day, when Hill was just a few shots off the lead, he was again invited to the pressroom. But he declined the invitation and told the reporters, "You were rude to me yesterday, and now I'm returning the favor." And he went into the bar and ordered a drink.

One reporter who'd stayed the day before came in, and Hill called him over and went over his round with the man. Then a man from a Miami paper came in and started asking Hill loaded questions—about his suit with the PGA, and about the U.S. Open in Chaska. "I told him to go ask the PGA about my suit. And I reminded him that Chaska was three-year-old garbage. He said something, and I said, 'Mister, can you read?' And he said yes, he could. I told him, 'Well, why don't you go buy a friggin' paper from Minnesota in 1970 and read what I said. And then go write your goddam story, because it ain't gonna be worth a shit anyhow.' And the next day, there was a story in his paper about what an ingrate I was. Hell, I don't care what they say. I don't read most of it. I don't care what they think."

And then he thought on it. "Well, I guess I'd like to win a major championship. I'd like to win a U.S. Open. Because they don't remember you if you don't win a major championship, and I'm like the next guy. Hell, I wanna be remembered."

16

It's Only a Tournament?

One of the best ways to get remembered is to win the U.S. Open. There is a certain mystique that surrounds the Masters, but the U.S. Open is more than forty years older than the Masters, and the oldest tournament in America and the toughest tournament in the world. Its traditions go back to 1895, when Horace Rawlins won in thirty-six holes at Newport Golf Club in Rhode Island. The Open is run by the USGA, and even some of the top professionals have to go through district qualifying to get in. One of the greatest things about the tournament is that it actually *is* open. Any amateur with a certified handicap of two or better is allowed to try to qualify in the sectionals and in the districts. The tournament moves to a new course every year, the USGA selecting new sites years in advance to give the clubs time to prepare and to toughen the courses almost to the point of being unfair. The U.S. Open is probably the greatest test of golfing skill—and luck—in the world. There is an awe surrounding the Open, a sense of importance that even the Masters can't come close to matching.

Even before one U.S. Open ends, they're talking about the next one. The courses are supposed to be the greatest courses in the U.S., and the golfers fantasize about and speculate on how the next one might play. In the off-season, the golf journals preview what the next Open course will be like, which will be the toughest holes, and what sort of player will be likely to win it. By the time it's June and Open time, even the best pros are afraid of the course. U.S. Open courses have similar characteristics: they have fast greens, so fast and baked and shaved that they're almost unfair. A player can touch a putt as soft as he'd touch the bottom of a hot steam iron and the putt might roll sixty feet. Even the best stroker can misjudge an undulation and miss by fifteen or twenty feet to the left or the right. (In 1973 Charlie Sifford, one of the better putters on the tour, six-putted an Open green).

If the greens can make even the best player look like a nine-hole hacker, the roughs can make him look even worse: the fairways are so narrow that Ben Hogan once remarked after a practice round at one Open, "We had to walk single file." The rough is so high and so thick that it's like playing out of tall patches of steel wool. The holes are long and the bunkers are huge and the pin placements are tricky.

The fringe around the greens isn't fringe at all but long grass, and the sand in the bunkers is usually new sand, which means the ball is more likely to bury.

The scrambler is better off back home eating beer nuts and watching it on TV.

Rod Curl didn't think he'd ever win a U.S. Open. It wasn't that he didn't have confidence in his abilities, but the Open courses were usually made for left-to-right hitters who could hit the ball low and play out of heavy rough and big traps. Curl's long suit was hitting the ball right to left—hooking it—and he was a good-lie player and not a great bunker player. It would be easier for him to win a tournament like the Masters, which was played on a high-ball hitters course built for a left-to-right hitter, or maybe a British Open or a PGA. And yet, as mediocre as his record was in U.S. Opens, the Open was still the tournament that inspired him the most. Whenever he played in an Open, he thought about all of the history behind it and was affected by the special feelings the Open seemed to inspire.

At every Open, the amateur and professional historians talk about Bobby Jones' four Open wins, or about how Jack Fleck, an obscure driving range pro from Davenport, Iowa, in a true Cinderella story, caught the great Hogan and beat him in an eighteen-hole play-off in 1955. They talk about Arnie's win at Cherry Hills, or they talk about all the other times Arnie *didn't* win. In fact, very seldom does somebody *win* the U.S. Open—usually, somebody else *loses* it. And every year, when June comes around, the story of Ken Venturi's win in 1964 is retold. After several very successful seasons, Venturi pinched a nerve and nearly paralyzed his right side in 1962, and his golf game left him. In 1964, he was almost broke—even the shirt company he'd been getting royalties from canceled its contract. His game was gone, his faith was gone, his confidence was gone and his money was gone. He was so desolate that the week before the '64 Open, he won $3,000 and he and his wife cried for joy.

The '64 Open was played at Congressional Country Club in Washington, D.C., and Venturi had to qualify in the districts. In those days the Open was played in three days—eighteen holes on Thursday, eighteen on Friday and, as a test of endurance, thirty-six on Saturday. By the time the double-round came on Saturday, most of the fans watching in their homes were rooting for Venturi. His 66 in the morning round had put him in second place, two shots back of Tommy Jacobs. But it looked as if victory was going to slip away from him, and that he might not even finish. Venturi was sick, dehydrated and exhausted. The temperature was up over 100 degrees and he'd nearly fainted during the morning round. Between rounds, Venturi was put under a doctor's care, and the doctor urged him to quit. But Venturi said he'd die before he withdrew. So the doctor went with him on the course, and Venturi staggered up and down the hills in the heat. He ate salt pills and many times he nearly fainted. The doctor pleaded with him to withdraw. But somehow he was able to finish, and even more unbelievably, to play under par and come to the last hole needing to make a ten-foot putt to win. White from dehydration, he stroked the putt in the hole, dropped his putter, looked up in the air and said, "My God, I've won the Open."

Venturi's great comeback would make him rich from books, articles and endorsements. Winning the U.S. Open under most any circumstances could mean a fortune in side money.

The 1973 Open was at Oakmont Country Club in Pennsylvania, where Arnie had lost to Nicklaus in 1962. Rod Curl missed the cut, but he stayed around and watched an unbelievable finish.

What most everybody had been expecting that week was that Jack Nicklaus would join Willie Anderson, Bobby Jones and Ben Hogan as a four-time Open champ. Nicklaus could handle the hard, fast greens and the high rough and the tight fairways. Nicklaus opened with a 71, then shot 69. But the third day he shot 74. He was still in the running, but the spotlight had turned to Arnold, who'd put a 68 with his two 71's and was tied for the lead at three under par.

Johnny Miller went to the tee seemingly out of it, having shot 76 the day before. He teed off an hour ahead of the leaders, with almost no gallery following him. The Oakmont people had intended to have hard greens, but there had been a lot of rain that week, and the greens were soft by Sunday. For Miller that day, it was like throwing darts. He birdied the first two holes, but he was still four shots back of the leaders.

He birdied the third, then he birdied the fourth. Suddenly, Miller's name appeared on the leaderboards at −1, but hardly anyone thought much about his chances. They were watching Palmer and Tom Weiskopf, Jerry Heard, Trevino, Julius Boros and John Schlee.

Miller three-putted the eighth but birdied the ninth, making the turn in thirty-two, something you're not supposed to do on U.S. Open courses. He birdied the eleventh, then birdied the twelfth from fifteen feet. He was six under for the day and three under for the tournament.

He birdied the par-three thirteenth with a four-iron to within six feet, then birdied the fifteenth with a four-iron to within ten feet. He was eight under for the day, five under for the tournament. And he fully realized that he could par in for a 63. He knew that if he blew it, he'd go down in history as a choker, no matter what else he ever did. He nearly birdied the seventeenth, then rimmed his putt for 62 on the eighteenth.

He had shot 32–31 for a 63 on an Open course. It was a record, and was being called, with justification, the greatest eighteen holes ever played.

The clean-cut young Mormon would become an almost instant millionaire because of his Open win, because millions of people saw that 63 at Oakmont on television. He owed it all to that little red light up there on the tower.

17

Stick Around— You Could Be in the Showcase

Higher, higher," they yelled in the front row.
"Lower, lower," they screamed from the back.
"Go for the car!"
"Take the box!"
"Door number two!"

In the living room of his house in Waterloo, Iowa, Tim Schmit switched the channel off that game show rerun in an attempt to find the station carrying the final round of the American Golf Classic on ABC.

Since Tim Schmit, Bob Starbuck, Roger Mastain, Mike Brogan and Gary St. John were in high school they'd been planning to go out on the golf tour to caddie. They knew that soon everyone would be going his own way, getting married, finishing college. They were waiting for the tour to swing through Iowa for the Quad Cities Open, which would not be for three more months. Until then they would be content to watch the tournaments on TV.

TV was that gadget, as A.J. Liebling said in *The Sweet Science,* "utilized in the sale of beer and razor blades." But that same gadget that hyped beer and razor blades had nonetheless elevated pro golfers to the status of celebrities and had inflated the prize money to the point of absurdity.

Back in the 1950's, ABC realized that they had a weak news image and decided to build elsewhere. That *elsewhere* was sports, and the TV impact made major spectator sports even out of such things as demolition derbies and wrist-wrestling championships. There were advertising millions waiting at the end of the tunnel, and the networks competed with such innovations as slow motion, the instant replay and the isolated camera. That intense competition for viewers ushered in the current era of the "challenge match," making possible promotions for obscene amounts of prize money—a tennis match, for instance, in which the loser made more than a quarter of a million dollars in one afternoon, surely a great morale booster to some jobless wretch who'd spent the week beating the streets for work.

Networks do golf shows mainly for the prestige of televising them and to build viewing habits, because a golf show, with its budget into the hundreds of thousands, isn't in itself tremendously profitable.

In the two planning trips to Akron, Ohio, for the American Golf Classic telecast, ABC had planned where its cables and towers and cameras would be placed, where the trailers would be and where it would house its people.

The weekend before the telecast, the equipment crew and the technical crew came to town to set up and bury the cable and put up the towers. They rented fork-lifts for the fairway cameras. The fork-lifts make a lot of noise when they move, which disturbs the golfers. So once the fork-lifts were set, they couldn't be raised or lowered.

There had been long-range viewer surveys made

by the network for this telecast. Over the years there have been certain methods developed for the basics of a telecast, but when a network goes to a course where it has never done a tournament, it has to do a lot of planning. It can't interfere with the golf shots, so if it has to run cable across the fairways and tees, it will have to bury it.

The technical crews had checked in and practically filled the Ramada Inn South near the golf course. The production people came in on Wednesday and checked into a downtown motel. Chuck Howard, ABC's head producer, didn't make the trip. Instead, twenty-four-year-old Terry Jastrow was handling the producing. Had Jastrow not decided to go to a golf tournament his sophomore year in college, he might've been out there playing instead of producing the telecast.

Jastrow had been a medalist in the National Junior in 1966 and lost to Lanny Wadkins in the finals. That same season, he beat John Mahaffey in the finals of the Texas State Junior, then got a grant to play golf at the University of Houston. When he went out to the Houston Champions tournament his sophomore year, they hired him as a spotter. He got more and more involved with television and less and less involved with his golf game. He would go to tournaments and football games as an announcer's assistant and researcher for ABC while he was in college. As soon as he was graduated from Houston, he had a job waiting for him as a production assistant with ABC. When he was twenty-two, he produced his first show.

ABC had held its production meeting on Friday afternoon in Akron. The show would go on the air for two days—one hour on Saturday and two hours on Sunday. Saturday morning, the pace was fast and Jastrow was on the phone for an hour talking to Chuck

Howard in New York. There were few jokes today. Crushed Coke cups and cigarette butts were all around the production trailers.

Close tabs were kept on the weather forecast. There was enough dead time in a golf telecast as it was, but rain delays were absolute disasters. ABC had taped material of interviews with pros, highlights of recent tournaments and swing sequences of top players, in case something like that happened.

ABC had sent around small video-tape cameras to tape the highlights of contenders on the front nine, since they wouldn't likely be up to the TV holes at air time.

Forrest Fezler had shot 67 to share the first round lead, then shot a 65 for a four-shot lead on Friday. ABC didn't want a runaway, unless, of course, it was somebody like Palmer or Nicklaus. Saturday's show went off well. There had even been a promise of some drama for Sunday when Fezler missed a five-footer for a birdie. If he'd made the putt, he would've had a three-shot lead, which would've given him a cushion were he to get in early trouble Sunday. And if he would've got off to a good start Sunday, with that three-shot cushion, it would've been hard to catch him. But going into the final round, he had only a two-shot lead over Tom Weiskopf, and three over Bruce Crampton.

Jastrow was in the tape truck Sunday morning with a spotter. They had taped swings of some of the top players for Dave Marr and Byron Nelson to analyze on the air if there was enough lag in the action to give them time to do it.

"Get Miller Barber," Jastrow said as the video tape rewound.

"Which one's Barber?" The man at the controls scratched his head. "They all look alike."

A technician listening to an earphone put it down.

"The Barber is always the one with the striped balls."

They ran the tape back and Jastrow clocked the swing sequence with a stopwatch, had an outline of the sequence typed up and sent to Marr and Nelson. Nelson would be on eighteen tower with Chris Schenkel. Marr would be on the tower at sixteen. Dave Diles was on the fifteenth, Bud Palmer was on the seventeenth, and Bill Fleming was roaming sixteen, seventeen, and eighteen fairways.

Before the telecast, Jastrow sat at the controls in the production booth watching the six monitor sets previewing the holes. Golf telecasts are snap-judgment dilemmas. Jastrow had to decide whether to show Jack Nicklaus three shots back and putting for a birdie, or to go over to Forrest Fezler, the leader, hitting a fairway shot. Most other sports have the action centered and cornered, but nobody's sure where it will be on a golf course.

And although the TV cameras can transmit the drama, they can't give the viewer the real idea of the difficulty of the golf courses the pros play. The viewers can't see the undulations in the greens or get a real perspective on how narrow the fairways are or how high and tough the rough is. It's not a long trip in the imagination from the municipal park courses to the pro tour. Someone who grows up playing the same easy course day after day for years and finally gets so he can shoot 70 on it might reason that it's not much more of a chore to shoot 70 on the pro courses.

Firestone Country Club was over seven thousand yards long, with narrow fairways, high rough, fast greens and a lot of sand. And what made the course play tougher was that it was almost all uphill and 100 percent carry to the elevated greens.

The commentators had written down statistics about the golf course and notes about the golfers to aid in their commentary. In the tower at the six-

teenth, Dave Marr had note cards with information
about some of the players, which he had jotted down
that morning.

JIM COLBERT
KANSAS STATE U.
HARD WORKER, WELL LIKED

JERRY HEARD. FRESNO STATE.
TROUT FISHES. RAISES QUARTER HORSES.
GOOD PRESSURE PLAYER.

BOB MURPHY, $105,000 AND TWO WINS AS ROOKIE.
ONE OF BEST POOL PLAYERS ON TOUR.

Dave Marr had most of his information in his
head, since he had played the tour for more than
fifteen years. He was the son of a club pro in Texas
and a cousin to Jackie Burke, Jr., who was one of the
greatest players in the world in the 1950's, when he
won the Masters and the PGA in 1956. As a small boy,
Marr didn't have much interest in golf. He liked football, but besides being little he was also rather slow.
He played in a junior tournament and won a small
prize as runner-up in the last flight. "I think every
time you win a little prize of some kind," he said, "it
stimulates you a little bit, if for no other reason than
it's one time you didn't get your brains beat out at
something." After his father died, when Dave was
fourteen, he worked around a pro shop in Houston,
played golf, and turned pro in 1953. "My family
needed money. My whole objective was to be a club
pro, because I'd never played that well."

He worked and lived at a club in New Jersey in
1953 at the age of nineteen. "It was actually an old
barn that had been converted into a clubhouse, and I
had a room back behind the golf shop in the rear
basement of the clubhouse. My room was only about

ten by ten, but it was as tall as the barn was. So it looked like I was living in a silo. The light fixture was fifty feet above my head, and I always felt like I was under a microscope."

Marr lived ten miles from town, and he didn't have a car, so it was a very lonely and not very glamorous New Jersey summer.

He tried the winter tours from 1957 to 1960, when there still weren't many full-time players. Most pros still had club jobs in the spring and summer. And there weren't many young players because the young players were working and saving up to go out and play the tour.

Marr made $1,900 for a third-place finish at LA in 1957. "I remember sitting there and saying, 'My God, nineteen hundred *gross.*' I taught all summer and didn't make nineteen hundred. And in four days at something I liked to do!"

In 1960 he decided that after having done everything else a pro was supposed to do, he should find out if he could play. He won $13,000 that first season, which was a pretty successful season in those days, and he won the Sam Snead Festival, which convinced him he could play well enough to make a career of the tour. The next season he won the Greater Seattle Open, and the year after that he won the Azalea Open.

"Then, in 1964, I finished second in the Masters to Arnold Palmer. But the thing was, I was playing with Arnold that last day and I got a lot of time on national television, which is maybe the strongest thing there is. People remember you from TV and your face becomes familiar. And I won a check that week for ten thousand dollars, which was far and away the biggest check I'd ever made."

In 1965 he won the PGA Championship at Laurel Valley. It was the last year that the PGA Champion-

ship meant a lifetime exemption to every tournament. "It was everything I could've hoped for. I never
thought I'd be a great player. I thought that my strong
suit was being able to be with people, and I didn't
want golf to be the end-all of my life. I wanted to be
with good people and bright people who make you
think a little bit. I mean, there's a lot more going on
in the world than the American Golf Classic this
week. I thought of golf as a way to get me to other
things. I'd always thought of it that way. I get tired of
most of the guys on the tour, who when you ask them
how they are they say, 'Well, I three-putted the eighth
green.' Of course, that may leave you with age, too.
But anyway, that same year I won the CBS Golf Classic with Tommy Jacobs, and those two things both
being nationally televised gave me a tremendous
amount of exposure. There was an article in a golf
magazine about me, which was wrong, about how I
won the PGA and lived royally thereafter. That PGA
was simply a means to go sell myself to the public."

He lived in New York City at that time. "A lot of
people thought I was crazy to live there, but New
York was where things happened, especially for athletes, and there weren't many golfers around New
York. I met a lot of great people who helped me with
different companies or to do commercials or to make
speeches. There are a lot of things to be said for hanging around New York."

Marr didn't win a tournament after 1965, but his
career was already in gear, and he had laid his
groundwork in many commercial ways. In 1970 ABC
asked him to get involved with its telecasts, to add a
little something to the show. For the first few years he
would play in the tournaments, and if ABC was tele-
casting, he'd come to the tower if he missed a cut or
if he played early. Later, he decided to stop playing in
the tournaments that ABC would telecast, and by 1975

he was a full-time ABC golf commentator.

"Where I can help the home viewer is to be able to tell him what sort of shot the player's got and whether he can play that sort of shot. It might call for a hook and he can't handle the hook. It's nothing to say that he's got a hundred thirty-five yards to the green, he's hitting an eight-iron and it's a shot over a trap. The point is, Is he a good short-iron player? And if the pin is in the right, is that to his advantage or disadvantage?

"Or maybe he's in the trees. Is his best way out of the trees *up* or *down?* That's something I should be able to spot. You can almost look at a guy and tell what his strong suit is. If he looks *up* first for a way out, you know he's not a good low-ball hitter."

Marr has seen television change the game, and TV has given him more opportunities than he ever believed he would have.

"Looking back to the early times," he said, "I wasn't making a lot of money, but I was still happy with the life. I liked the traveling and I liked to drive. We'd go out of our way to see the Royal Gorge or to go to Tombstone or to some alligator farm in Florida, or to Judge Roy Bean's place in Langtry, Texas. At that point there were fewer guys on the tour, fewer outside distractions, and it was simpler. Luckily and thankfully, I've been successful, but you have more demands on your time. You have less time to stop to see Langtry, Texas, or some alligator farm, because you're flying over them. You're going to shoot an ad for Jantzen, or Allied Chemical wants you for a VIP outing, or you're doing an exhibition for some company, or doing what I'm doing right now. You have what you've worked for, but you have less and less of your own personal time. And I suppose you don't have to go *out* to see all of the wonders of the world— television keeps bringing them *in.*"

While Marr was on the tower at sixteen, Jastrow was in the production trailer checking his watch and glancing up at the monitor sets. Over in the graphics trailer they worked fast, putting names on a rotating cylindrical drum, pulling numbers from boxes marked POSITIVE NUMBERS and NEGATIVE NUMBERS, looking at charts of every player's rounds, charts which showed where each player made birdies, eagles, bogies and pars. The names and numbers of the leaders would be superimposed onto the screen.

As they worked they could hear Jastrow over their headsets. "Mac, show me Johnny Miller. Where's Miller, Mac? Okay. Now, Bobby, show me Palmer on a line at fifteen tee. Graphics, what does Nicklaus stand for the day?"

"Minus one," graphics reported back.

"Dorrance," Jastrow said. "The clothing charts aren't up close to the cameras. At least the cameramen are saying they don't have it."

Dorrance Smith called for a runner for the clothing charts.

"I need sixteen fairway hitting order, Bobby," Jastrow said. "Has the last group putted out on thirteen?"

"They just finished," the voice reported back.

"Okay, everybody," Jastrow said. And he started counting down. "Ten . . . nine . . . eight . . ."

The viewers at home saw an aerial view of Firestone Country Club as soft music played, and in the production trailer Jastrow said, "Okay, *go,*" and they were on the air.

The voice-over on the aerial shot was that of Chris Schenkel, who welcomed the audience to Firestone Country Club. "It's the final round of the American Golf Classic. This ABC sports exclusive is brought to you by . . . the Firestone Tire and Rubber Company. By . . . Chevrolet. Chevrolet makes sense for America. And by . . . Acushnet, makers of Titleist golf balls and clubs. We're out to improve your game."

In his headset while he talked, Schenkel could hear Jastrow. "Straighten the leaderboard, Dorrance. David Marr? Somebody knocked it into the water on sixteen, so let's lateral into that water hazard there. He'll be playing four. Yeah, Chris, you can just go at your leisure. Smoothly, but at your leisure. They'll follow you. All I can say, gentlemen, is that there are millions of people in China who don't care. Let's make this an entertainment show, not a documentary. Jimmy, stand by for a commercial right here at the head. . . . . . And . . . *leaderboard."*

The leaderboard flashed on the main screen, and Schenkel was saying, "—where Forrest Fezler has lost a three-shot lead to Bruce Crampton."

Fezler had been double-trapped on the first hole and bogied it. He was playing right behind Crampton, where he could see Crampton birdie the second, fourth and sixth to take the lead. ABC had made a tape showing Fezler double-bogie the eighth hole, and it was being shown to the viewers. They were being told that Crampton now had a three-shot lead.

They cut to Marr to talk about the four televised holes while Jastrow looked at the other monitors. "—And the sixteenth," Marr was saying, "a six-hundred-twenty-five yard par-five that cannot be reached in two. What makes this hole interesting is that the third shot is over a lake that runs up to the edge of the green." He pointed at a model of the hole with his baton.

"When he's done, Chris," Jastrow said, "we'll take a commercial lead-in."

If there had been TV when Lindbergh made his famous flight, he might be forever remembered doing coffee testimonials or grinning down at the economy-size bag of Bow-Wow dog food as if it were the landing strip at Le Bourget.

Without the TV money in golf, there wouldn't be the quality of play there is today.

The network pays the tournament a flat fee for the rights to televise the tournament, and a certain percentage of the network profits goes to the TPD, which keeps 30 percent of that money and puts the other 70 percent into a TV package fund. The money in the package fund goes to all of the tournaments according to the amount of their prize money and whether or not they're televised.

While the commercial ran, they searched frantically for John Mahaffey's name in the graphics trailer.

"Dorrance," Jastrow called. "Where's Mahaffey on the leaderboard?"

Dorrance yelled out to the back of the trailer, *"Come on, goddammit, Harry.* What the hell you doing? We got a John Mahaffey there? Well, put his ass back up on the leaderboard."

"Okay," Jastrow said as the commercial ended and New York got ready to cut back to Akron. "Ready on the hole-model piece? Lead to the hole-model piece, Chris. Stand by, David Marr. Five . . . four . . . three . . . two . . . one . . . *go, Chris."*

The viewers saw a blimp's-eye view of fifteen, and heard Schenkel say, "To get an idea of this great golf course, take a look from high above." And soft music played background to the aerial shot of the rolling fairways.

"Leave the super in there for a lot longer," Jastrow said. "Feed camera two to slow-mo. Record Crampton. Get the mat in, Mac. Just leave it in, leave it in." He was sweating down into his shirt now. "All right, now fifteen tee hitting order, Bobby. Get me the hitting order. We'll come to seventeen tee after Weiskopf and Crampton hit. Good chance to establish—hitting order on fifteen? Crampton first? Any delay? Stand by on slow motion, Merrit."

"You want normal speed, Terry?"

"Yeah. Let's go to the birdie putt. Stand by."

Because Crampton had a three-shot lead, the commentators had to go to a lot of color and talk about how important second place was. They went to Marr and to Byron Nelson's tip for the day.

As the end finally neared, the tension increased in the graphics trailer. "Goddam sonofabitch, will you, goddammit. Get it up there, get it up there."

Finally, Bruce Crampton came to the eighteenth, and the cameraman got a close-up of him hitting his second shot to eighteen. The ball rose up and flew to the pin. It takes a good cameraman to follow the shot and catch the drama of the ball hitting and biting near the pin or falling in a trap or splashing in the water hazard.

As they neared the close, Jastrow's voice sounded weaker. The people in the graphics trailer were sweating and tired. Crampton walked to the green and the crowd cheered. Schenkel told the viewers what was coming up on *The American Sportsman* and got ready for his close.

He had three closes, and which one he would use depended on the time left. His *long close* had a list of audio credits, his *short close* said simply, "The executive producer of ABC Sports is Roone Arledge. Today's coverage of the American Golf Classic was produced by Terry Jastrow and directed by Mac Hemion, technical directors Werner Gunther and Bill Morris," and then a list of the commentators and a plug for the sponsors.

"Fifty-five seconds," Jastrow said, squeezing an empty Coke cup. "You'll have to go to the panic close, Chris."

They just got Crampton's last putt as Jastrow counted down, "Fifteen . . . fourteen . . . thirteen," and Schenkel said, "Once again, the winner of the American Golf Classic is Bruce Crampton. Ground Transportation provided by the Chevrolet Motor Division. The preceding was a presentation of ABC Sports, recognized around the world as the leader in sports television."

A scorekeeper in the graphics trailer plopped down in a fold-out chair, dropped his arms and hung his head.

Terry Jastrow opened his clenched fist and a crushed Coke cup dropped to the floor. He let out a long sigh. The show was over.

18

A Million-Dollar Baby in a Five-and-Ten-Cent Store

Rod Curl had made the cut and $425 at the American Golf Classic, but he was falling out of the top sixty. The tour moved to Chicago for the Western Open, and the $600 he made kept him in sixtieth. He had made nearly $25,000, which would've been enough to be leading the women's tour, which was moving into Chicago as the men headed for Milwaukee. Not exactly *into* Chicago. Midlane Country Club, where the Ladies Professional Golf Association tournament had been scheduled, was in Wadsworth, Illinois, closer to Wisconsin than to Chicago—a long-distance telephone call from downtown.

There were very few grown trees on the Midlane course, and the wind blew hard almost constantly. It was a new course, and the women were being used to publicize the course and possibly attract the members it would need. They were playing in the $35,000 Child and Family Services Open. The tournament had been publicized as being in Chicago, very likely because few people would have known in what part of Illinois Wadsworth was located.

The LPGA was used to this. If the men's tour was the three-ring circus, the women's tour was a sort of small-town carnival with a tilt-a-whirl and the octopus ride, fool-the-guesser, a couple of games of chance. But things were changing. There had been little prize money in the 1940's and 1950's. The lady pros probably could've made more money teaching elementary school, and they couldn't have made much doing that either. In the 1940's and 1950's most of the women who went out to play in the LPGA looked a lot like men, but could scarcely play like them.

By the 1960's the national golf boom had reached the housewives, and there were more and more schoolgirls who could really play the game and were liberated enough to go on the road and try to make a living at it.

The 1960's brought more prize money too. TV brought it, and the feminist movement in part began to change the way women's athletics were viewed.

Arnold Palmer had been the right man at the right time. In the 1970's it looked as if the LPGA might've found the right girl at the right time. Her name was Laura Baugh, the glamour girl they lacked, a girl who looked like a star and played like one.

She was the proverbial million-dollar baby in the five-and-ten-cent store. Dimples. Blue eyes. Charm. A little Shirley Temple smile and bows and ribbons in her hair. Blond hair, five foot five, 115 pounds, bouncing down the fairways, blinking at the press, breaking 70.

Laura Baugh grew up playing golf, won the National Pee-Wee five times, the Junior World title, the California Girl's championship twice, the LA Women's City championship three times, and in 1971 at the age of sixteen she won the U.S. Women's Amateur.

And Mark McCormack saw green in little Laura's blue eyes. He signed her before she turned eighteen, and while she was waiting for that birthday so she could get her LPGA card, McCormack hustled up enough contracts and exhibitions so she could make $100,000 in six months. She played in Japan and signed with a car company and toured Europe with her golf game.

When she got her card, she nearly won the first tournament she played in, finishing a shot back in a tie for second. With McCormack's commercial hand to guide her, she got a contract as an instructional editor with *Golf* magazine, which put her picture on their October 1973 issue with the caption SEX PLUS SOCK. They called her "The Sweetheart of the Fairways," and she looked the part.

As far as sex appeal is concerned, one might be more drawn to Jan Stephenson or Sandra Post or Sally Little or JoAnn Washam, among others. Laura has a sort of All-American-Girl-Next-Door sexiness. But it is marketable. She has contracts with a car company, two magazines, a watch company, a resort in Florida and another in California, and the Bermuda Tourist Bureau; she plays golf matches in Japan, and is featured there on a "Laura Baugh Calendar" (one picture for every two months). And while McCormack blitzes the market with a Laura Baugh publicity campaign, the galleries and the press have taken to her quickly. She plays an excitable, emotional game, jumps up and down when she hits a good shot, smiles and winks and waves to the galleries. Some tour girls resent the fact that she can be doing worse and draw twice the crowd that they can, or that the press walks by the leaders to talk to Laura. But, as with Palmer in the sixties, when Laura Baugh's price goes up, it raises the other girls' prices. And the advertising people are aware that these girls are good for selling toothpaste, detergent, cars, real estate, vacation packages and just about anything else.

Years ago, had you described the typical woman pro, you would've likely had an image of a girl with fat legs and short hair who wore long skirts and looked more like a Marine drill instructor than a lot of Marine drill instructors. And there was that lesbian thing. There were probably a lot of straight girls who were scared to try the tour. And there *were* some lesbians out there, and probably still are. But as one of the caddies who follows the LPGA circuit says, it doesn't make any difference.

"A lot of girls out here got just as much man in 'em as me and you," he said. "Probably had as many women as me and you. But I'll tell you this, they're the ones who treat us the best. Them half-men, or whatever you want to call 'em, they pay you better and they treat you better. Don't ask me why. It's just that way."

Whenever two girls travel together, somebody is sure to whisper things about them. Men on the tour travel together and nobody says much about it. But women pros go into strange towns and have to stick together for self-preservation as well as for financial reasons.

Laura Baugh was a refreshing sex symbol for the LPGA. "I guess sex appeal is part of the overall public appeal," she said. "I try to be, you know, fashion-conscious, and I watch my weight. And I try never to wear an outfit again once I've been photographed in it."

Viewing Laura Baugh as a sex symbol isn't so much sexism as hard reality. Women can't compete on the golf course with male pros and they realize it. And when you hit the ball 220 yards and shoot 75, you had better come up with something. A sex symbol who can shoot low numbers isn't a bad start—a woman who is pleasing to look at and still worth following eighteen holes purely on the merits of her golf game.

In the 1960's, a lot of women got involved with golf because they liked the way Arnie hitched his pants or smiled at the galleries, or the way Doug Sanders dressed. Later, they got involved with the golf itself.

When a person goes to a men's tournament, he sees the best golf there is, so the women have to come up with some extra added attractions if they hope to compete for the fans. The physical thing isn't enough. They still have to be able to play. Sharron Moran came out on the women's tour in 1967 after getting the *Golf Digest* award as "Most Beautiful Golfer." She had all the looks and dressed in style, and she had an awful lot of heart and desire, but she couldn't hit it far enough or well enough to make it on the tour, or to bring the galleries pouring into the gates.

Laura can.

There are other girls out there now who also can. JoAnn Washam is five three and looks good. She can also average 240 to 250 yards on her drives and break 70. She joined the LPGA tour in 1973, at the age of twenty-three.

"I don't mind being called sexy," she said. "It's a compliment. It may depend on who says it and why, of course. That doesn't bother me. It does bother me if someone writes an article and describes me, the way one woman did, as 'a petite little thing' all the way through the article, and never once mention my abilities on a golf course. As long as the physical appearance is just a sidelight, then it's great."

JoAnn played in boys' junior tournaments and was captain of the boys' high school golf team her senior year back in her home state of Washington. "I knew most of the golfers in the area and I'd got some recognition, so most of the boys weren't shocked to see me on the golf team. The guys on my team were great. So were most of the guys on opposing teams. The back-handed remarks came mostly from the visiting coaches."

JoAnn made only $6,000 her rookie year, but after learning to adjust to the grind, she made close to $20,000 and finished thirty-second her sophomore season, which was comparable to winning about $80,000 on the men's tour.

"We're not strong enough to compete *against* men," she said, "but you might see us playing *with* the men players. They used to have the Haig and Haig tournament, which was a good tournament, where men and women pros played together. Maybe we'll have tournaments like that in the future."

The 1960's had brought better golfers out to play in the LPGA. Mickey Wright, the great Kathy Whitworth, Carol Mann, Mary Mills, Susie Maxwell Berning, Jo Ann Prentice, Donna Caponi Young, Sandra Palmer, Judy Rankin, Sandra Haynie and several more. But the glamour came in the 1970's. And it's on Laura Baugh's shoulders that the burden rides and the banner flies. She works hard on her game, and McCormack sells her with his huge publicity network. TV is running out of new places and Madison Avenue is always looking for new faces.

In 1960 Louise Suggs led the LPGA tour with $16,892. As recently as 1970, Kathy Whitworth led it with just over $30,000. But in 1974, Laura's second year on the tour, JoAnne Carner made over $87,000, and Jane Blalock made $86,000. Betsy Cullen, the eighteenth leading money-winner in 1974, made as much as Kathy Whitworth had led the tour with just four seasons before.

And there was, of course, Colgate-Palmolive, who gave the LPGA its first $100,000 tournament in 1972, the Colgate–Dinah Shore Winner's Circle Open. In 1973 the tournament was worth $150,000. In 1975 it was worth over $200,000 and was the LPGA's version of the Masters.

There are still plenty of $35,000 tournaments on the LPGA circuit, but the trend is upward. The LPGA players know they have to try harder, and they treat the press and the public better. And there are no ropes to keep the people off the fairways—they can walk right alongside.

And a good many of them will be walking right alongside Laura Baugh. While Laura can go first-class, a lot of the other girls can't. It's still a financial struggle. The sixtieth woman player in 1974 made exactly $5,071.25, and probably used the twenty-five cents to do her own laundry. It's hard to set up a drivable tour, because it's hard for the LPGA to get tournaments where and when they want. The LPGA, however, does contact people in private homes near the courses, usually club members, who let the girls who need it stay free at their homes.

It's hard for the women to get sponsors, because it's a bad risk. "There probably aren't fifty women out here who have sponsors," JoAnn Washam said. She sponsors herself. "About the most luxurious thing I do is send my laundry out. And to play good golf, you have to curtail your social life. I get a little down sometimes because of the routine, but there are a lot of routines that are worse. It's hard work, but it's a nice, unregimented way of life if you can make it, and if that's what you want."

There will be more and more girls who will come out to try that sort of life. The LPGA tour will change and grow and get its share of the runoff of leisure money.

That day at Midlane Country Club, Laura Baugh came into the grill and talked to three sportswriters from the Chicago papers and one from a national magazine.

Two heavy-hocked women players sat mostly unnoticed at one of the corner tables eating cheeseburgers and bowls of chili.

Laura ordered a Diet-Rite.

19

Lajoie Chews Red Devil—Ask Him If He Don't!

As June moved toward July and the tour left Milwaukee, Curl dropped out of the top sixty for the first depressing time since back in February. Almost half of the $25,000 he'd made had gone to expenses. Most of the players who had sponsors didn't have to worry so much about expenses.

John Jacobs *never* worried about expenses. Even if he was broke, he wouldn't worry about expenses. When he was twenty-three, he decided to try the tour. He had his own bankroll, but a wealthy sportsman offered him an extra $7,000 to take along just to spend and never pay back. Jacobs declined at first, but the man insisted. Jacobs called his best friend, John Nichols, and asked him if he wanted to go with him, and even with Jacobs's bankroll and the extra $7,000 *and* the $1,200 John averaged every week in winnings, they were destitute inside of three months—bumming cigarettes and eating celery.

They had tipped cabbies $10 to take them down the street. They had left $5 tips with $2 tabs and had

155

bought champagne for people they didn't even like.

For his first five seasons on the tour John Jacobs had had more sponsors than the Johnny Carson show.

Having somewhat matured, Jacobs had cut his sponsors down to two men—his southern California sponsor and his northern California sponsor. His southern California sponsor was Ray Kawano, his good friend and owner of a large produce company; his northern California sponsor was Syl Enea, a very wealthy land developer who owned, among other things, a country club near Oakland, and who had been like a father to Jacobs since Jacobs' own father had died in 1967.

When he was home in California, Jacobs and Kawano played a lot of golf together and now and then went to the race track. If Enea's club had a dinner or something special going on, Jacobs would be available to help out when he wasn't playing the tour.

In the locker room at Milwaukee, Curl had been figuring his expenses and talking with Bob Wynn about how to cut corners. Jacobs sat down at their table and Curl asked him what his expenses came to for a season. Jacobs answered, very seriously, "Rod, if I watch myself, I can get by on about fifty thousand a year." The season before that, Jacobs had made about half that.

In Bob Wynn's first year on the tour he had sold shares of himself and had raised $8,000 to play in thirteen tournaments. He won $5,200. The next year it was, again, anybody who cared to donate. At the end of the second year anything that was left over was to be divided up. He played in thirty-two tournaments that year and made $13,000, and there was nothing left over. The next year, 1972, he came up with a single sponsor, a man named Henry Harlow who owned a trucking firm in Dayton, Ohio, which hauled prefab homes across country. Every week, Harlow would put money in Wynn's account to cover all the expenses, but the nice thing about their agreement for Wynn was that he got a percentage off the top from any check he made. For the first two years of their agreement, Wynn was a business loss for Harlow.

But Wynn helped out in other ways. He would keep in touch with Harlow every week by phone and call on him whenever he went back to Dayton. They would fly somewhere to make calls on Harlow's accounts, and they would play golf with the accounts and take them to dinner, which helped Harlow with his business and enabled Wynn to meet people who might help him someday.

Not all sponsor arrangements were as good as Bob Wynn's. Some backers were in it strictly for the gain, and some others were in it just for the excitement of being a part of the scene.

Before the 1960's, there were fewer sponsors. Even today, with more prize money, the worst investment a man could make—next to a Broadway play—would be to back a professional golfer.

When Dave Hill first joined the tour in 1959, at the age of twenty-one, he made an agreement with a man who agreed to back him. When he got to the Texas Open, the lady at the registration desk told him that his check wouldn't be honored, that without so much as a warning to Hill the man had decided to drop him. Hill didn't have enough money to keep playing, so he and his wife drove back to Michigan, thirty-six hours in the blizzard, which convinced Hill that from that point on he should sponsor himself.

In 1972 Joe Porter had gone to see a fight between Muhammad Ali and Jerry Quarry on closed-circuit TV in Cleveland. When he left the auditorium where the fight had been shown, three thieves jumped him, and he broke his shoulder and had to crawl to his car.

He spent what he'd saved to play the tour during the twelve weeks it took him to heal his shoulder injury. He went to Ohio to get his car and play in a satellite event in hopes of making enough to keep going. He made only $200, enough to get him back home to Phoenix.

On his way home, however, he ran into a man who backed several golfers on the tour. The man, Lincoln Pierce, who owned a plumbing-equipment wholesale supply house in Indianapolis, at first decided he couldn't back Porter, but later changed his mind and bankrolled him.

Sometimes the promoters and business agents who've got involved with the game put up the money for the players' expenses.

Although Sam Snead and a few others had lawyers helping them, back before the big money got to the game, Mark McCormack was probably the first fulltime golf manager. He started with Arnold Palmer, then got Jack Nicklaus and Gary Player, and by the 1970's he had done so well that he had offices in cities all across the world and handled basketball players, tennis players, skiers, race drivers and even iceskaters. He had a literary department just to deal with all the books and magazine articles his athletes would be involved in. When a writer would do a book with Arnold Palmer, for instance, he would have to barter for his percentage of the profits, and very often half the profits would go to Palmer, a third of the profits would go to McCormack, and just 17 percent would go to the writer. His firm retained outside investment advisers to manage the athletes' money and to generate income for them.

Managers and promoters are in charge of everything from hyping a golfer to the public to setting up exhibitions and spots in private pro-ams and speaking engagements and endorsements. Some managers go so far as to make arrangements with magazines to pay plane fares or hotels for writers sent to do pieces on their athletes.

In exchange for all their labor, the managers usually get 20 percent of everything they generate for the golfers. They might handle legal work, taxes, accounting, maybe even handle all the itinerary at tournaments for the golfers, in exchange for a fee. Some managers talk the golfers into giving them 20 percent of what they make on the golf course, but most golfers won't be talked into such a thing. There are golfers who have signed contracts in which they are so bound that they have to accept every deal the managers make for them, which means that if the manager says to jump up and down on a mattress on national television, they're bound to do so.

TV has opened up a whole new frontier for Madison Avenue and the pro golfers, whose faces are now so familiar to viewers. The athletes have become symbols—credible liaisons between product maker and consumer. This isn't anything totally new, however. Back at the turn of the century, the Queen City Tobacco Company ran ads using Nap Lajoie, the Cleveland baseball star. The ads said simply: LAJOIE CHEWS RED DEVIL TOBACCO. ASK HIM IF HE DON'T!

Rube Waddell, a pitcher during the same period, was notorious for drinking stuff a lot harder than Coca-Cola, but Coca-Cola featured an ad that quoted Waddell: "More than once, a bottle of your Coca-Cola has pulled me through a tight game. There is nothing better for pitchers in hot weather. I find Coca-Cola stimulating both to body and mind and is the only beverage of the kind .that does not leave an after effect. In every game I work, I keep a bottle or two on the bench for an emergency, and I can say that Coca-Cola has never yet failed me."

It seems almost ridiculous to talk about ethics in

advertising because it is often a sell-out to begin with. But there *are* limitations. As soon as Johnny Miller finished second in the 1971 Masters, his manager had already set him up with enough contracts to make Miller a millionaire. But as soon as Miller won the U.S. Open, Miller Beer wanted to associate their Miller with Johnny Miller, and the contract had to be passed over because Miller is a Mormon and Mormons don't drink.

To use athletes to get the attention of the buyers seems legitimate enough, but the underlying message is always that if a person uses the same products as some star athlete, it will somehow make a better man of him, or make him play golf or tennis better. Lee Trevino is no more of an expert on aspirins— probably much less so—than Nap Lajoie was on chewing tobacco. And Arnold Palmer is no more qualified to judge the ride of an expensive automobile than is any gas-pump attendant or door-to-door vendor.

So while the golfers thought about their shots, the managers thought about how the golfers would look in a new brand of double-knits, or if their smiles would sell toothpaste or station wagons. And the fat ones who couldn't sell clothes might be peddled to do testimonials for front-end alignments and transmission work.

Curl knew that if he ever started winning tournaments, he could make a lot of side money because of his size and because he was an Indian. He and Wynn talked about it in the locker room that day.

Right now, however, Curl was more worried about survival than side money. His game still wasn't coming back, and he didn't know what to do about it.

Somebody mentioned that the Amana Refrigeration Company paid players to wear Amana caps during tournaments; there were even bonuses for winning. George Archer and Bob Goalby actually listed Amana, Iowa, as their home course, although Archer lived in Gilroy, California, and Goalby in Belleville, Illinois. A reporter killing time in the locker room that afternoon said that Archer and Goalby must have had Amish shopkeepers out there shagging for them, because there wasn't even a golf course in Amana, Iowa.

Bob Wynn shook his head and looked out the window. "You know," he said, "someday somebody's gonna come out here and tee it up nude."

20

Das Kapital

Curl was still out of the top sixty as the country celebrated the Fourth of July. He made two cuts in a row, but he was still out of the top sixty going into the Canadian Open. In the first two and a half months of the season, he'd made close to $20,000. In the next four and a half months, when he should've been getting better, he made less than $9,000. He made $750 at the Canadian Open, and he felt like he was getting his putter going again.

He liked the Westchester course the next week. The club itself was a very stuffy one, not far from New York City—"Members only" on the patio, that sort of thing. Inside the clubhouse there was a painting of John McEntee Bowman, the founder of the Westchester Biltmore Country Club, and the caption inscribed below the painting said, "Exponent and patron of clean sport."

This was old money, and there was even a stockbroker's office in the clubhouse, so that people at the tournament were drawn between the leaderboard and the exchange board at Ernest and Company.

Curl and his caddie had been having their problems, arguing about yardages and club selection. It had been a long hard summer and it was showing. Curl had a good week in Westchester. He shot 72–69–72–69 and won $1,353. He didn't move up in the standings, though. He just held his position. He was in sixty-second place, behind Bruce Devlin and Allen Miller.

He called home that Sunday night after Westchester to find out how things were going there. He missed his kids, and Suzanne wanted him to come home. He told her he had to stay out there to make money, but she said "We don't need money," and after he thought about it, he wished he'd said something else. He didn't think it was such a good idea to be pumping into a little kid's head how important money was.

But on the exemption list, it was very important. And Curl had to sit out during the PGA, which made him edgy. The PGA Championship was different from all the other tournaments; players got into that tournament on the basis of the money they'd won on the tour from one PGA to the next. The PGA still belonged to the club pros—it was basically their tournament—and club pros from different regions around the country could get into the tournament by qualifying, although touring pros were admitted only by the official money they'd won.

The PGA, like the U.S. Open, was moved around each year. It was first played at Siwanoy Country Club in Bronxville, New York, in 1916. At that time it was the first tournament in the United States of any consequence that was solely for professionals. James M. Barnes won one up in match play over Jock Hutchison in 1916.

Lionel Hebert won the last PGA championship that was match play. That was in 1957, and it gave him a lifetime exemption to play in any tournament he wished. In 1965 Dave Marr's win at Laurel Valley in Pennsylvania was the last time the PGA would be a lifetime exemption. From that time on, winners of the PGA would be exempt from qualifying for ten years after they won.

In 1972 the TPD passed a rule that would permit the top fifty lifetime money-winners to have three-year exemptions, to be taken whenever they needed them. The rule was supposed to protect a good player who was a drawing card and who had been injured or sick the season before and had finished out of the top sixty. But what happened was that a lot of the older players who weren't playing good golf anymore were able to take tournament spots away from younger players with more ability.

Joe Porter was one of the players who fought the top-fifty lifetime rule. "We fought the damn thing with petitions. We had a hundred seventy-five signatures. They were mostly non-exempt players who signed, because why would exempt players even care? The tour's controlled by the top twenty money-winners anyway. They're in control of all of the boards and committees. It ought to be run by all the players. The Tournament Policy Board is made up of businessmen and they're pretty much controlled by the top money-winners."

The PGA champions and Tournament Players Championship winners and U.S. Open winners all get ten-year exemptions from qualifying.

"You don't see guys who hit four hundred in baseball get a lifetime contract," Porter said. "Bob Lunn had a couple of good years in the sixties, and now when he's making five thousand a year, he gets a three-year exemption. How many people come to tournaments to see Doug Ford or Jerry Barber? When a ball player can't play anymore, he gets pushed out by younger players who are better. That's what makes it a sport. All the exemption rule does is take a spot away from a young guy who can play better. They've had their chance, now they ought to give us ours." Porter shook his head. "Hell, why don't they just have a ten-year exemption for every guy who wins a tournament, and about twenty-five weeks after next year there won't be any qualifying spots left."

Some players tried to get the TPD to take some of the money off the top in the tournament payoffs and put it farther down. Some of the players, mostly those who weren't cutting it on the tour, wanted the TPD to have two tournaments a week in different cities. Half of the top money-winners would be forced to play in one tournament, the other half in the other. Nobody paid that much mind.

But there are arguments for taking some of the prize money and moving it down. The winner of a tournament gets 20 percent of the total purse, and the man in second gets 11.4 percent.

"If a tournament is worth forty thousand to the winner," Porter said, "and if he wins two or three very early in the season, he starts to sit out and take more time off. This hurts the tournaments that can't put up more than two hundred thousand dollars in prize money, even though they're good tournaments on good golf courses. You don't have to put the money all the way down to the bottom, but if you're a tournament sponsor, you want the winners there because they're your drawing card."

There is some truth to that. In 1974 Jim Dent played in nearly forty tournaments, and so did Jerry McGee and Frank Beard. But Johnny Miller played in only twenty-two, Nicklaus in only eighteen, and Gary Player in only fifteen.

The tour players split into two camps on the money issue. Some players saw arguments on both sides. Leonard Thompson, for one, was quite vocally against moving the money down. "The guys who are trying to change the tour," he said, "the guys who want to take all the prize money and put it down at the bottom, are guys who can't make a damn dime out here. Some of them are friends of mine. But they want to fix it so you can come out here and play half-assed golf and make twenty-five thousand a year. They want somebody to *give* 'em a living. Hell, if you're an accountant and you can't do your job, they fire you and get somebody else who can. It's cold . . . but that's the way it is."

21

The Return of an Old Friend

Curl had watched the PGA on TV in his motel in Sutton, Massachusetts, where he waited for the next tournament. He had found himself silently rooting for Arnold Palmer at the first of the week. Even those players who didn't care for Palmer personally seemed to appreciate him as a golf hero and would root for him in the PGA, the one major championship he'd never won. But Arnie missed the cut and Nicklaus won the tournament.

During July, Curl had felt his game creeping back. He had started hitting it straight, playing with more consistency and more confidence, and putting better. He had worked hard that week in Sutton while the PGA was being played in Ohio.

The week of the USI Classic in Sutton was a wild week for the caddies. Three of them had made the acquaintance of a nymphomaniac in Canada, and they took up a collection to pay her plane ticket to Sutton. Before the week was over, she had worn down most of the caddies, a couple of rookies and one veteran, and the caddies had gone to the truck stops to seek aid, bringing back eager Red Ball, Navajo and Pacific Intermountain Express drivers to take care of her.

On Sunday the marshalls caught her over near the seventeenth fairway going at it right in broad daylight with one of the caddies back in the trees, and they threw the two of them off the golf course. The next day she went home, and the caddies felt as if they'd lost a real friend.

Curl won $903 at Sutton and moved into sixty-first place. The next week, he was playing in the Liggett & Myers Open in Cary, North Carolina, when his golf game came back to him in one round.

Curl had opened up with a 72, five shots off the lead, then shot 70 the next day to make the cut. He let a good round get away from him on Saturday, shooting a 74 instead of the 67 or 68 he thought he should've shot. But the important thing was that he felt it was there, that he had it again. He hadn't had it going well since way back in the first two rounds at Jacksonville in March. But now, on the twenty-sixth of August, he started making birdies.

He eagled both par-fives on the front side. He birdied the eleventh, twelth, thirteenth, fourteenth and fifteenth.

After he hit his shot on seventeen, one of the caddies ran up to the practice green. "The Indian's shooting the spots off the ball," he said. "Got it eight under and he just put a shot dick-long on seventeen."

Curl felt as if he was in a trance when he teed off on eighteen. He hit a good drive, and then he came out of the trance when he checked the leaderboard. He realized he could win the tournament. Bert Greene and Miller Barber were fighting for the lead at six-under for the tournament. All Curl had to do to shoot 63 was to par the eighteenth. He'd started the day three over par, and now he was five under. But he knew that if he parred the hole the best he might get was a tie for second or third. That would be good money, and he needed the money. And all he had to do to par the hole was to play for the fat of the green, avoid the bunker on the left where the pin was, and two-putt. But if he could make birdie, he knew that he might end up in a play-off for the whole thing. And as hot as he was, he might even make his second shot and win it all with an eagle. First prize was $20,000, second was $11,400 and third was $7,000. Playing safe might make him an extra thousand or two, but he knew that you had to push your luck when you were getting it. It seemed like a good time to gamble. There was a big difference between playing safe and smart, and not having the guts to play your cards when you were getting them. He decided to go for it.

He was so pumped up that the biggest thing he had to fear was hitting the ball too far. He hit his second shot and it started hooking, but it hooked a little too much and ended up in the trap. There was hardly any room between his ball and the pin, and his blast shot went ten feet by, his putt rimmed the cup and he made bogie.

But he'd done it the right way. Greene and Barber tied at 278, and Greene won in a play-off. Curl's 64 was a course record, and it had put him at 280, which tied him for fifth place. Still he'd been right. Playing safe might've made him another thousand or so, but a birdie would've given him a 62, a total of 278 and a chance to play off for first prize. He was glad he'd at least given it a run.

He left Cary, North Carolina, with $4,000, which put him in fifty-seventh place with just ten tournaments to play. He was $565.01 ahead of sixtieth place, but he was leaving North Carolina with a new attitude, new confidence and a golf game that had disappeared in the spring, had stayed away all summer and had come sneaking back over the Carolina pines like an old friend.

He flew first-class to Hartford.

22

Grinding

It was muggy and hot in Hartford that week, and the caddies came in rubber-legged after every round. Curl shot 72 the first day, then shot 65. The third day he shot 66 and was just three shots off lead. The game was fun again. But the last day the rains came and the wind blew, there was a lightning storm, and when it was gone, Curl's game had absconded—at least temporarily. He shot 77 and made only $355. A good day might possibly have cinched the top sixty for him. As it was, he dropped down to fifty-ninth place, $410 ahead of David Graham in sixtieth.

It was hot again the next week in Columbus, Georgia, for the Southern Open. It was a terrible time to be in that part of the world. It was so hot that even 80 degrees would seem like 100—and it was in the high 90's all week. For the third time that year, Forrest Fezler finished second. He was getting a reputation for finishing second, which was, if nothing else, better than getting a reputation for finishing third.

Curl scratched for every shot at the Southern

Open, shot 72–72–71–70, won $401 and hung onto fifty-ninth place. He was hitting the ball well but he just couldn't seem to get it into the hole. All week he lipped putts and missed birdie opportunities which might have given him the momentum to shoot some great rounds.

Going into the Sea Pines Heritage Classic on Hilton Head Island, South Carolina, Curl was exactly $235,496.41 behind the leading money-winner, Bruce Crampton, who might well have paid his caddies nearly as much as Rod Curl had made for the season. The Harbourtown golf course, where the Heritage was played, was one of the toughest courses on the tour. Curl shot 75–71–72–71 and made $868.25. But Jerry McGee had tied for sixth and won $5,100, and Curl dropped down to sixty-first place, just over $400 out of sixtieth. A lot of crazy things could happen down the stretch. Anybody could get hot, finish with a couple of seconds and thirds and end up bumping you out of the top sixty.

Curl still felt that his game was there. If he could just put it together down the stretch, he could make it.

Curl liked the course at Bettendorf and the course at King's Island, where the tour would soon be, and he counted on making good checks there, maybe cinching the top sixty with a little luck. It was getting to be hunting season in California now. There would be deer all over Shasta County near his home, and there would be elk near his sister's on the Modoc Reservation up near the Oregon border. But he had to keep grinding. He worked hard on his putting and watched Nicklaus, Trevino and Johnny Miller to observe their technique. He'd always been able to pick things up by watching the good players.

The tour moved to Broome County, New York, for the B.C. Open, and Curl opened with a 69, four shots off the lead. There was a fog delay the next day, which Curl had gone into with birdies and had come out of with bogies. He shot 70 and made the cut. There was fog again on Saturday, and Curl shot 70. He was in position to make a good check. He played it smart on Sunday, didn't try anything wild, and came in with a 72. That tied him for eighteenth place and won him $1,200. But it didn't move him up a notch in the standings. He was still in sixty-first place, just over $400 behind Steve Melnyk, as the tour headed for Bettendorf and Rod Curl headed down the stretch drive for that top sixty.

Part 3
THE STRETCH

23

Welcome to Bettendorf: Iowa's Most Exciting City

Tim Schmit, Roger Mastain, Mike Brogan, Bob Starbuck and Gary St. John had been waiting four years to caddie on the tour. They had waited until the tour hit Bettendorf, Iowa, for the Quad Cities Open, for two reasons. Bettendorf was only a hundred and thirty miles from their hometown, Waterloo, and if things didn't pan out, it wouldn't be a long trip back; and they had been under the impression that tour caddie jobs would be hard to come by in the summer with a lot of college kids out there.

When they got to Crow Valley Country Club in Bettendorf, where the tournament was to be played, they were told that the best way to line up caddie jobs was to talk to the caddie-master, who would be there the next day for the Monday qualifying round. They were also told that a lot of tour caddies, just as the rumor had it, wouldn't make the trip from New York to Bettendorf. The tour caddies, many of them weary from a long season, were looking for a week off. The Quad Cities Open was only a $100,000 tournament, and the tour would be heading for Ohio the next week. Rather than make the trip to Iowa from New York, where the tour was, many of the more successful tour caddies would spend the week in New York, then pick the tour up back in Ohio. The rumor was of much comfort to the Waterloo brigade, who pitched their Sears Roebuck tent on a hillside near the fourth fairway, told stories, speculated on life outside the borders of Iowa, and drank beer until the last few were warm and foamed when they popped the tops.

They all got jobs on Monday caddying for rabbits, but Gary St. John's man, Bob Shaw, had tendinitis. Shaw picked up after three holes and Gary was out of a job.

That night they made a tour of the nearby beer taverns and pizza joints, and were eating pizza when a storm kicked up. It rained so hard that they couldn't see out the window of the pizza house, could barely see out the windshield of their limo, and couldn't see their tent at all. And then they realized why they couldn't see their tent. The rainstorm had blown it down completely. Their sleeping bags were soaked, and they had to head for a motel. Most of the motels were full, and they had to race a car from the Ramada to the Tall Corn Motel for the last room. They signed in as a twosome, hung up their wet sleeping bags and slept two in one bed and three in the other.

Gary St. John figured he was screwed. He was the only one who didn't have a job, and all Tuesday morning it had been a washout for him. He sat down near the pro shop to smoke a cigarette, and the caddie-master came and got him. He would have a job with Mac McLendon. Gary had walked off the yardages twice, and he gave his yardage card to McLendon, then they played a practice round.

When the practice round was over, Mac told him to grab that bag of shag balls and come over to the practice tee. "You ever shag before?" he said.

Gary had never shagged before. Usually the golf courses furnished practice balls and the caddies didn't need to shag because the balls were picked up with a machine. But some clubs didn't furnish practice balls, and the pros would have to hit their own. And the caddies would have to stand out there and shag them.

Shagging was terror. It was overcast and there were more than thirty caddies out there—and even worse, more than thirty pros on the practice tee hitting shots. It wasn't so bad at nine-iron range, but it got worse as he moved back. It was so overcast that he couldn't see the balls until they were almost right on top of him. He was scared somebody would skull one and it would hit him in the head and kill him.

Golf balls dropped like mortar shells in a Grade B war movie. Gary would try to catch Mac's shots in the bag, but he'd miss most of the time and he'd have to go hunt for some of them in the tall grass while all around him he could hear balls landing. Most of the other caddies were terrified too, especially the local caddies who'd never done it before. Every time a voice on the tee would call, "Okay, come on in," a chorus of caddies would yell out, "Me? Me? You mean me?"

Some of the caddies wouldn't show up the next day.

Leonard Thompson walked onto the practice tee, and Mac stopped hitting to talk to him. Gary let out a deep breath. *Maybe he wouldn't hit anymore.* Then Mac motioned to Gary and Gary pointed to the clubhouse, but Mac waved that off. He cupped his hands over his mouth and yelled out, "Leonard's gonna hit some of mine. Watch for two balls at a time."

When Mac finally called him in, Gary ran all the way.

All of the boys from Waterloo got jobs working the pro-am on Wednesday. Only Gary's man was playing in the pro-am. The other boys worked for amateurs. Tim Schmit carried doubles in the morning, then doubles again in the afternoon and made $45. His afternoon job was murder. One fellow had a big duck-hook and the other fellow had a bad slice, and he spent the whole day running from one side of the deep rough to the other.

Rod Curl got to play in the pro-am because a lot of the top names were skipping Bettendorf. There was only $100,000 in it, and they had grown accustomed to $200,000 and $250,000. Curl liked this course because the greens were fast and tricky, he was a good putter, and that would give him an advantage. The year before, he'd shot a 65 the last day, tied for ninth and won $2,600.

It was overcast again on Thursday and the course was wet from heavy rains the night before. The greens wouldn't be as fast and tricky, but they still would be faster than the average greens. Curl was satisfied with the way he played on Thursday. He shot 69 and lipped a couple putts. He was five shots off the lead.

The boys from Waterloo found out that caddying for weekend players in Waterloo was a long way from caddying on the tour. There was no rest. As the last man was hitting they had to start walking just as his driver cracked the ball. They would have to put the bag down next to their player's ball and start looking for the sprinkler head or whatever they'd used as a yardage marker, determine the yardage and talk it over with the player. When the player would hit, the caddie would have to replace the divot, clean the club while he walked fast and then try to catch up to the player before he got to the green so he could give him his putter. The caddie would have to clean his man's ball and give it back to him, then tend the pin while he putted. After his man putted, the caddie would have to hustle off to the next tee and do it all again. It was like that all day, and it was wet and hard to walk up and down the steep hills.

Friday morning the fog was so heavy that there was a delay until it began to lift. The first groups teed off barely able to see their drives land. Curl was in one of the early groups. He shot 70, but was still seven shots off the lead. He had made the cut by three shots. He wished the greens would dry out and get faster, because he figured he still had a couple of good rounds in him for this course.

If the caddies had found shagging tough the day before, it was even worse in the fog. Sometimes they couldn't see the balls fall at all—they could just hear them. They were afraid to duck because they might duck into one, and they were afraid to move because they might move into one. None of the caddies wanted to go hunt for balls. Every caddie was stealing everybody else's balls and none of them cared. In the afternoon, the fog lifted and it got as muggy as a steam bath.

It rained hard again Friday night and the course couldn't be cut Saturday morning. The pros normally had to play the ball as it lay, but since the course hadn't been cut, the TPD officials allowed them to clean their balls in the fairway and place them back down on all of the holes except the par-threes.

Curl played another solid round on Saturday and came in with a 69, and this moved him up some. There were a lot of players who could shoot one good round or two good rounds, but if you shot three good rounds in a row, you were sure to move up close to the top. He knew that if he could shoot the same kind of round the next day, he could win at least $1,500.

Sunday was finally a nice Iowa autumn day, but the wind kicked up in the afternoon and blew hard. Curl didn't mind the wind because it didn't slow down the powerful hook he usually played. The greens were faster, and Curl started making putts. He birdied the last three holes for a 67, then waited for the finish to see where he'd be.

Sam Adams, one of the few lefties on the tour, had shot back-to-back 64's on Friday and Saturday, and he came down eighteen fairway with a lot of the tour rabbits cheering him on from the sidelines. He shot 68 and won by three shots. A few weeks before, he had been worried about losing his card. Now he was a tournament winner and would get everything that went with it.

"I made a lot of friends on Mondays," he told the press. "I'll miss the friends. I won't miss the Mondays."

Dwight Nevil had finished in a tie for second and won $9,200. The week before, Nevil had finished second all alone to Hubie Green and won $11,400. Nevil was a short, muscular fellow from Texas, and had once been a fireman in Dallas. He had made a run for the top sixty the year before, his second year on the tour, but he fizzled out late in the season. Before the B.C. Open two weeks before, he had been in eighty-fifth place on the exemption list. The finish at the B.C. shot him up to sixty-eighth place. And now, the finish at the Quad Cities shot him up to fifty-first place, with just six tournaments to play.

For the second year in a row, Curl had tied for ninth at the Quad Cities Open, and his $2,142.86 moved him back into the top sixty. He was in fifty-seventh place, but only $726 ahead of sixtieth. He would catch a plane to Cincinnati. He had the Merc back now. They had even fixed the front end, and it was running pretty well. His caddie would drive it to the Ohio King's Island Open.

The tour caddies were leery of local caddies and didn't mix much with them. They weren't unfriendly, but they kept to themselves. But when a magazine writer swiped sandwiches from the press room and gave them to some of the tour caddies, a black tour caddie gave one to Tim.

Of the contingent from Waterloo, only Roger Mastain's man and Gary St. John's man had made the cut, and just barely. Gary made $130 for the week, and Mac asked him to work for him again at King's Island.

Tim Schmit had spent Sunday trying to line up a job for King's Island, but to no avail. He found Rod Curl packing his car in the parking lot and he said, "Aren't you Rod Curl?"

Curl said that he was, and Tim asked him for a job for the next week. Curl explained his situation, that he was trying for the top sixty and he needed a caddie with a lot of experience—a tour caddie.

"I'm a tour caddie," Tim said.

"You are?" Curl said. "How come I've never seen you at the tournaments?"

Tim paused a long, theatrical pause, tugged at his beard and pulled his shoulder-length hair away from his face and said, "Oh, you probably just don't recognize me since I got my hair cut."

Curl liked that one. He told him maybe somewhere down the line.

The members out by the gate were drinking kegs of beer in a trailer, and they offered some to the boys from Waterloo. The fun was over for the members, and it was back to the routine for them. It was shading toward dark when the boys pulled their pallbearers' car out of the gate and headed toward I-80 east. There was an even greater excitement to leaving a town than coming into one.

There was a sign near the entrance to I-80 that read: WELCOME TO BETTENDORF, IOWA'S MOST EXCITING CITY. They decided that that sign must've been put up there by the state to avoid overpopulation.

It was over four hundred miles to Cincinnati.

24

Tour Caddies and Proud of It

They hit I-74 off I-80, and headed south through Peoria. Bob Starbuck had agreed to drive it straight through, but after about 50 miles he got tired and Tim Schmit had to take it. Twenty miles outside Indianapolis, when he couldn't drive another mile, Tim pulled over to a rest stop. Gary and Roger woke up and slid Tim over. Gary drove. He chain-smoked cigarettes to help him keep awake. He tried sticking his head out the window for fresh air. Finally he stopped for gas and coffee. It was a cut-rate station that featured a REGULAR and a THRIFTY, which they were leery of.

Next to the station was a little truck stop where a fat woman served food and took plates from a long, hairy tattooed arm that would hand the orders through a small window to the kitchen. Gary heard clanking noises that sounded as if they were coming from the kitchen. The man could've been back there fixing tires. The rest room was dirty and somebody had penciled above the urinal: *Red Ball Drivers Can't Go The Route!*

It was five in the morning when they finally got to Cincinnati. They had never been to such a city before, a place that had its own major league baseball team. They went out of their way to find the stadium just so they could say they saw it.

The Ohio King's Island Open was being played at the Jack Nicklaus Golf Center, about thirty miles outside Cincinnati in a little town called Mason. Nicklaus was part owner of the course and he was also the designer. The course had been built directly across the street from the King's Island amusement center, which was a park on the order of a Disneyland. Next to the golf course was the King's Island Inn. Tim Schmit checked on how much it would cost them to stay there, and when he found out that the price they gave him was for one night instead of the whole week, he and his friends headed for a nearby campground and pitched their tent.

They were all hungry, but caddies weren't allowed in the clubhouse and they couldn't get anything to eat. They looked for jobs for the qualifying round and for the week.

By nine in the morning it was raining hard, and at eleven the TPD officials decided to cancel the qualifying round and hold it on Tuesday. The rain stopped just past noon and it cleared off.

The boys from Waterloo hung around in the afternoon hunting for jobs, but by three o'clock, they still hadn't come up with anything.

They were the only ones sitting in the caddie tent when the caddie-master's phone rang. Tim picked it up and said hello. A voice on the other end asked if this was the caddie-master. Tim lowered his voice. "Uh, yes, this is the caddie-master. What can I do for you?"

"We've got four players up here who don't have

caddies. Bob Erickson, Jim Simons, Ben Kern and John Jacobs."

Tim didn't know who any of them was, but he didn't care. "You just send them right down here and we'll take care of them."

When the players came down, Tim told them the boys had been assigned to them, and they now all had jobs except Roger, who was back in the tent sleeping.

At the office of the campground they talked to the fellow who ran the place with his wife. He was like an old bartender. He had all sorts of stories about who had been there before, about some guy from Kansas City in '67 who'd mooched off him, and different guys who'd leaned on his shoulder. The man seemed to like the boys, and he said he envied them for what they were doing. He put them on a free-water hookup, and told them how to trip the dryers so they wouldn't have to pay. He gave them pop and put some frozen pizzas in the microwave oven and fed them. They ate pizza, drank pop and talked to the man and his wife until very late that night.

Though the tour caddies had been leery of them in Bettendorf, some of them recognized the boys the next day and spoke to them or nodded. Dwight Nevil's caddie, Chuck, saw Roger sitting around the tent Tuesday afternoon and asked him if he had a job. Roger said no, he couldn't find one, and Chuck took him over and introduced him to a player named Bob Payne, and Roger had a job. The tour caddies realized that they were going to stay on the tour and they accepted them now. J.C. Stewart, a black caddie, recognized Tim Schmit from the week before, and he talked with Tim about how to behave, where not to go around the courses, and how to act on the course. He said that if they ever had any questions to come and ask him. As an afterthought he advised Tim not to be loaning out money.

There were breakfast rolls out that day for the caddies. Tim got a roll and read the sports page. That weekend the Cincinnati Bengals would be playing the rival Cleveland Browns, and the baseball season was coming down to the wire with the Reds in the battle. It wasn't an ideal time to be playing a golf tournament in that area, but it was the best date the tournament committee had been able to secure.

And then it rained again on Thursday and an electrical storm came up. The TPD officials suspended play, the players headed for the clubhouse and the caddies for the caddie tent.

The rain at a golf tournament always divides the players into two distinct camps—those who have played well and want the round to stand, and those who have played poorly and want to get it canceled.

"Just a fall shower," said one player who'd shot 69.

A player who was three under par with four holes to go said, "It'll burn right off."

"Hell," said a player who'd shot 79, "it's pitch-black up there. It's lightning. They can't force me to endanger my life out there. I don't think they can do that, and by God, I'll fight it all the way."

It went on like that for two hours while the fans were crowded into the clubhouse, the bar did a big business, and the players were jammed into the locker room. The TPD officials talked back and forth on their walkie-talkies, trying to decide what to do.

The players played cards, changed into dry clothes and told stories.

A pro from Texas said he'd been out late at one tournament because he'd had a late tee time the next day. He was going up to his motel room when he heard voices and stopped near the top of the stairs.

When he looked down the hall, there was one of the stars of the tour lying in the hall with some girl he'd picked up, some local hairdresser, and they were both so drunk that they were unable to get in the door, although they'd managed to get the key in and the door about half open. And right there in the middle of the hallway, the girl was humming her tune on him. The Texas pro walked right over them, but they didn't even notice him.

When the rain finally stopped, one of the players yelled, "Get those cows outta the stable. I'm ready to go."

But the TPD officials finally decided to cancel the round. None of the scores that had been posted would count. That was fine with Curl, because he had been two over par when the rain hit.

As it was, the 75 that Jack Nicklaus had shot was wiped out too. Nicklaus jumped on his good fortune, the way he usually did. He rarely shot two bad rounds in a row, and Friday proved no exception. Nicklaus, on his own layout, came in with a 68 and a share of the first-round lead.

Rod Curl took advantage of the second chance too. He shot 69 and was only a shot back.

Curl liked going to the press tent, because if you did this it usually meant that you were close to the lead. He went over his round with the reporters and told them how he'd made his birdies, bogies and pars. When he left he said, "I hope I see you guys tomorrow."

It was sunny on Saturday, and Curl's 71 put him in a tie for second place, three shots back of Nicklaus. In the press tent the reporters brought up the top sixty, and Curl talked about what it was like trying to get out of one circle and into a higher one. "You think about it all the time. You're always telling yourself what it means, and there's hardly a day this late in the season that you don't sit down and figure what it's gonna take to make it."

Tim Schmit had been surprised to hear his man, John Jacobs, say that he didn't particularly want to be in the top sixty. "You just have to be a bunch of places and do a bunch of things," John had said. Tim liked working for Jacobs—he would talk to Tim and let him in on all the stories and all the jokes. He liked working for Jacobs also because of the prestige. It made him feel important to walk up to Jacobs' ball, which would almost always be fifty to a hundred yards past everybody else's, and hear a fan or some marshal say, "Man, who you caddying for? I been here all day and nobody's even come close to hitting a drive that far."

Tim had heard Curtis Sifford tell a story about how back in his amateur days in Los Angeles he'd been putting out on a 400-yard hole. He heard a thump and a ball trickled up between his legs. He looked around to bawl out the guy who'd hit his second shot onto the green. He looked back and saw no one. He looked back and back and still saw no one. He finally spotted a tiny figure 400 yards away on the tee. "Nobody had to tell me who it was," Sifford said. "I knew it had to be J.J."

There was a light rain early Sunday morning, but it had stopped by ten o'clock. The crowds had been sizable on Saturday and they were sizable again on Sunday. And those who wisely followed the leader were treated to a spectacle—Nicklaus shot a nine-under-par 62 and equaled his best tour round ever. He would go into the last round of his own tournament leading by ten shots.

Curl's 70 had put him three under for the tournament and up near the top, only one shot out of second place, and second place would be more than $14,000 and would easily cinch the top sixty for him.

Nicklaus had such a big lead that only five thousand people came out on Monday for the final round.

Gary St. John's man, Mac McLendon, had barely made the cut, but by the fourteenth hole on Monday he was one under par and up among the leaders. Gary's eyes opened wide as he came to the fourteenth and looked at the leaderboard: MCLENDON −1.

Gary said, "Hey, there we are."

When McLendon put a wedge shot close on the eighteenth and people cheered, Gary walked along looking at the gallery and feeling important. Mac finished with a 69, and the kids asking for Mac's autograph off the eighteenth green were asking for Gary's too. He would sign his name right under Mac's. McLendon would finish in a five-way tie for tenth place and make $2,650. He had just over $20,000 for the season and was way back in ninety-seventh place. But he felt good. It was the best he'd placed for a long time, and he thought that if nothing else he could finish the season in a flurry and have a good taste in his mouth for the next season. He gave Gary $320 for the week. It was the most money Gary had ever made in one week in his life.

Curl had played it a little too cozy that last round and ended up with a 74. He knew he should've done better, but he had tied for seventh and won a very much needed $3,687.33, and he was counting every dime now. With five tournaments to go, he was in fifty-sixth place with an official $43,323.16, just over $3,000 ahead of Jerry McGee in sixtieth.

Everybody in the Waterloo outfit had jobs lined up for the next tournament. Because of the World Series, the TPD had not scheduled a tournament to try to foolishly compete with it. So the next week would be an open week; and the week after that, the tour would be in Napa, California, for the Kaiser Open.

They had plenty of money and plenty of time, so they decided to take their time going across country to Napa. They would stop back in Waterloo for a day and tell their adventure stories to the high school kids dying a slow death from boredom back in the high school hangouts.

They were *tour caddies* now, and proud of it.

25
Choking

When they stopped to visit in Waterloo, Gary St. John walked up to the pro shop at Porky's Red Carpet Club on Tuesday afternoon waving $300 in twenty-dollar bills. He threw the door open, held the money up and said, "Here we go, boys. I'm *rollin'.*" He was the big winner and the top man.

Their friends from Porky's Red Carpet Club formed a circle around them near the putting green and listened to their stories. Everybody wanted to know if they'd seen Nicklaus up close or what Arnie was really like, whom they were working for, and whether they had gotten laid.

They were the center of attraction, and their friends wanted to buy all the beer that night.

They left early the next morning. It would be two thousand miles to Napa from Waterloo.

Nebraska was such a flat, boring ride. There seemed to be very few trees west of Omaha and nothing to stop the wind from the Rocky Mountains except the ten-story buildings in Denver. They could see now what drove the pioneers so relentlessly westward. They ate in diners with honky-tonk music on the jukebox, and the truckers squinted at their long hair. They had debated on whether or not to stay over in Cheyenne, but Gary had never seen mountains before, so they pushed on. About twenty miles outside Cheyenne, Gary yelled, "Oh my God, look at those mountains."

"Those aren't mountains," Tim said. "Those are just foothills."

On the other side of Rawlins, Gary saw the big snow-capped Rockies stretching all the way to the horizon. He did not know how they would get over them. It looked as if they'd just drive right into them.

They drove all day, through Salt Lake and out into the alkali desert into Nevada. And late that night, when they were exhausted, they finally stopped in Elko.

Elko was a dirty little town. They wouldn't want to live there. They did, however, want to try one of the legal whorehouses they'd read about, but they never got around to it. They checked into a motel and went to a saloon that had slot machines. They all lost money. Roger lost the most—$50.

Roger Mastain was usually a late sleeper. Sometimes you'd have to pour water on him or drag him out of bed. But that next morning, he jumped out of bed at seven o'clock and threw on his clothes before anybody else even had his eyes open.

At the White Bear Casino, he lost on the slots and tried the blackjack tables. He lost at blackjack and headed for the crap tables. And after he lost there, he went to the Bix Six wheel to try to redeem his money. But when he reached down into his pocket, he didn't have any more cash. He started for the window to cash a traveler's check. He just didn't see *how* he could lose like that. On his way to the window a short, suspicious-looking fellow grabbed his elbow and said, "You need a good watch?" The man was sweating and had lost his tie somewhere.

When Roger went to the window, he looked back at the fellow, then stuck his traveler's checks back in his pocket and got out of there.

He had dropped $85 in less than an hour. He had lost almost $150 and he wasn't even halfway through Nevada yet. The others knew that he'd lost as soon as he walked in the door and they saw the look on his face.

As he packed he realized that he still had to spend a whole week in Las Vegas at the Sahara Invitational. "My God," he said. "I may have to take out a loan just to get through the week."

When your luck goes bad, it seems to stay that way. When Roger went out to try to start the car there was a slow grinding noise, slower, slower . . . and then nothing.

The cold wind blew dust into swirls across the highway as they pushed the big Pontiac. It couldn't be push-started, since it was an automatic, but there was a gas station down the road.

When they finally got there, the man said a new battery would cost them $22, which would include charging it and installing it. The gas station man ate mayonnaise from a huge jar with a big spoon. He was a strange fellow but he did good work, and they were back on the road in a little over an hour.

Roger made the others promise that they wouldn't let him out of the car in the State of Nevada except to go to the bathroom.

They finally got to Napa Sunday night. There was nowhere to pitch their tent, so they drove out near the golf course where the qualifying would be held, but they couldn't do it there either. The local police gave them permission to camp in an apple orchard next to the golf course. They bedded down in a gazebo next to the course.

They woke up to a clear sky and a warm sun. There was a flower garden next to the gazebo, and behind them were rolling hills of orchards, and the mountains beyond that, and off into the distance they could see ships sailing in and out of a big bay. But out on the golf course, the rabbits were already fighting it out for the spots that were open in the tournament.

Rod Curl had gone home to stay with some friends, since he didn't have a place of his own anymore. He visited with his folks and his brothers and he saw his kids every day. And every day he practiced all the shots he thought he'd need to take him down the stretch.

The practice seemed to help. On Thursday Curl opened up with a 66 and was in second place, one shot back of Grier Jones. He wanted to hold that position so he could make enough to jump out of the rat race and into the big time. He shot 72 on Friday and was six under par for the tournament, five shots out of the lead, and he stayed late to work on his chipping and putting.

He couldn't have asked for a more beautiful day than Saturday. And he birdied the first hole, bogied the sixth, birdied the tenth and twelfth and was two under for the day, eight under for the tournament. He parred thirteen and fourteen, then birdied fifteen and was three under for the day.

And then, trying to get a little too much on a drive, he turned his hands over too quickly, swung too fast and snap-hooked one out of bounds. That was a two-stroke penalty, and he double-bogied the hole. He hit the eighteenth in regulation, but three-putted for a bogie, and instead of a 67 or 68, he'd shot 72. It left a bad taste in his mouth.

On Sunday he got it going, and he came to the

fifteenth hole one under for the day and seven under for the tournament. And then he bogied, double-bogied and bogied for a 75. He'd choked it off both days and he knew it. He should've made four or five thousand dollars, but instead, he made $912.30.

One shot better and he would've made $1,000, three shots better and he would've won $2,500. If he'd just shot 70 that last round, which he knew he should've done, he would've won $5,000, shot up to forty-ninth place, and could've coasted into the top sixty from there.

He was so depressed when he left the golf course that he couldn't even talk. There was a pop bottle that kept rattling under his seat as he drove. He reached for it but couldn't get to it. Then he whipped over to the side of the road, got out, got the bottle, and took a run at a brick wall and threw the pop bottle as hard as he could. It hit the wall and shattered into little pieces.

Back at the motel he felt a little better. He wanted to get it out of his system, because he had learned a hard lesson many times, one that would be good to keep in mind the next week in Las Vegas—and that was: *Never chase your losses.*

Curl had dropped from fifty-sixth to fifty-eighth. There was $3,500 between him and sixtieth place, and four tournaments to go.

26

Las Vegas: For Sale–(Cheap) (For Cash)

The Las Vegas bookmakers don't make book on golf. It would be too hard to set the odds; golf really doesn't encourage that much betting; and it would be the easiest sport in the world in which to take a dive. There used to be a big legal Calcutta in Las Vegas before the Tournament of Champions was moved out of Vegas in 1964. The players were auctioned off to the highest bidders—a sort of parimutuel type of betting—and singer Frankie Laine won hundreds of thousands on Gene Littler when Littler won the Tournament of Champions three straight years.

Back when they played the first Tournament of Champions in 1953, there was legalized betting on it and the bookmakers gave odds. Al Besselink, a clutch player and a high rolling pro out of Grossinger, New York, found out that he was going off at 25–1. He bet $500 on himself to win. Besselink beat the favorites on the last hole the last day, collected the $10,000 first prize and picked up $12,000 more from the bookies.

The Sahara Invitational was the big tournament

in Las Vegas now. It was a poor cousin to the Tournament of Champions before the late Del Webb came to town in 1961. Webb was a land developer from Phoenix and a golf fanatic. In 1958 the Sahara Invitational was a 36-hole tournament with a $500 first prize. Two years after Webb arrived and bought the Sahara Hotel, the Sahara Invitational was a 72-hole tournament with $13,000 first prize.

One thing that Rod Curl liked about playing in Las Vegas was there was so much to do. At most tournaments, when he shot poorly, he couldn't seem to get his mind off his game. But in Las Vegas he could go to the crap tables and forget what had happened on the golf course.

The locker room at Sahara Country Club was crowded on Tuesday afternoon. Del Webb's pro-am lasted two days and was played on two courses, giving all the golfers a chance to play in it.

Bob Wynn had his feet up on the table checking his list of who owed him what. One of the rabbits tossed a $10 bill down on the table. "Cross me off your list."

"Friggin' Bengals are tough, aren't they?" Wynn smiled.

Curtis Sifford saw Ken Still coming into the locker room. *"Kenny Still.* You wanna go for some big dough today?"

Still grabbed a cold Coke from the cooler. "I'll take a team to win the Super Bowl for a hundred and you take a team to win the Super Bowl for a hundred."

"I thought you couldn't bet," Wynn said.

Still popped the top on the Coke. "As of October ninth I could start stackin' again."

"Why *then?*" Sifford said. "The commissioner make a new rule?"

"I lost five hundred on October ninth last year on a football game," Still said. He shook his head and laughed. "Hell, I cased the game, went to practices, the whole works. So I made a personal rule not to bet again for a year."

One player wanted to play Bob Wynn for a hundred dollars on nine holes. "I'll give you a lesson," he said to Wynn.

"The only friggin' lesson you could give me," Wynn laughed, "is a payin'-off lesson. Tell you what, though. I'll let you off for forty on the first tee. How's that?"

The TPD policy toward the players' gambling has been to ignore it. They couldn't do much about it anyway. A man has to have gambling blood in him to try the tour in the first place, because it takes almost $30,000 a year to play it. Most of the betting is done on baseball, football and basketball. Ten years or so ago the players used to bet big money on the course, but since the mid-1960's and the big prize money, the golf course gambling died down. Players like Palmer and Nicklaus, Trevino and Miller, are making so much money that they have no need to gamble on the course. Some of them have their regular games on Tuesdays during the practice rounds. But most of the big gambling is done by the rabbits, because they could use the extra money. But if they lose it on Tuesday, they're already in the hole when the tournament starts.

There used to be a few hustlers hanging around the tour trying to beat the pros out of their money, but now most of the men who would've been hustlers a few years ago are on the tour. The TPD ran the rest of them off.

Pete Brown used to play golf at Fox Hill in Los Angeles where a lot of big gambling went on. There he ran into a man known as Three-Iron Gates. "Three-Iron would play you with just his three-iron, and that's all," Brown said. "He'd putt with it and everything. He could hit the ball two-twenty with that thing. He'd put it on a big wet leaf, like a banana leaf, and the ball would fly off that thing and roll forever. He'd bet you whatever you wanted to bet that he could get down in two from a trap, just using the three-iron to get out with and to putt with."

George Johnson overheard Brown and said, "He could *bust* me then."

"He almost *did* bust me," Brown said.

"I won't bet on any trick games," Johnson said. "But I sure wish I could run into him now."

"Oh, he won't bet with you now. He's too old."

George rotated a Coke can in his big hands. "If he can stand in a bunker . . . and put it in with a three-iron in *two,* then he's *got* me. He can send me on to the poorhouse . . . and I'll be glad to go."

There was a lot of betting going on during the practice rounds in Vegas. The casino atmosphere had put them in the mood.

A caddie was telling Tim Schmit about how he had caddied for a pro who couldn't get gambling off his mind. "Man, he'd call Memphis from San Diego and lay down two grand. We were out West and the man actually found a phone smack in the middle of the golf course and called in a bet. He played the courses good out West, but he didn't like it out there because the time change screwed up his damn betting. After the West Coast, he was about one-hundredth on the money list, but if you added his gambling, the dude was in the top thirty."

John Jacobs laced his shoes near the clubhouse as he prepared to play a practice round. Tim asked him how he was doing on the tables. John looked at him in a very strange way and said, "Hell, I don't know."

Jacobs hadn't been playing well and he wanted to go home to California to get his brother Tommy to work on his swing. But he hadn't wanted to pass up the action in Las Vegas.

On his practice round, Jacobs got to speculating about what the tour would be like if everybody had to play for his own cash. "You always hear the TV commentators say, *'This putt is for seven thousand dollars.'* Like it was some big deal. Hell, it's somebody else's money. If the guy was going to *lose* seven thousand of his own cash, he'd be squeezing that putter a lot harder."

One of the caddies in their group said to Tim, "I'll bet if that dude ever wins a tournament, he'll rent out the suites and *do* the town."

Tim said, "I believe he does that already."

Jacobs told him that most of the big gambling was done when the pros come home off the tour, that there were always people back at the pros' home courses waiting to challenge them for money.

Tim and the others had checked into a cheap motel for thirty-seven dollars for the week, dirty walls, bad mattresses, chipped bathtub enamel and four towels for the five of them.

While Tim and Gary had been taking their things into the room, a short, cheerful, bald-headed fellow came up and started a conversation. His name was Preevo and he'd been in Las Vegas three years. He worked at a car wash and got government disability checks even though he looked the picture of health.

Preevo told them that three years before, he had been driving home from work on a Los Angeles freeway when a semi truck crowded him off the wrong exit. There was no entrance back onto the freeway, so he kept driving. He drove all the way to the El Cortez Casino in Las Vegas, got into a card game and won $3,200 and decided to stay. He no longer had the $3,200 and he no longer had the car, and though it was the middle of October, he still had a tan, except where his watch and his ring had recently been.

He hit them up for three dollars, a half-pack of Winstons and two double-edged blades, all of which they were sure they would never again see.

That night they drove down the Strip through the exploding neon. All of Fremont Street downtown glittered with the flash of switchblades in the pawn shop windows. In the windows of the shops and apartments were signs that read: FOR RENT . . . or FOR SALE (CHEAP) . . . or MONEY LOANED ON ANYTHING OF VALUE . . . and in one window, SEWING DONE CHEAP (FOR CASH).

Back down at the Strip, unable to find a clock, they asked a bellman in the Sahara what time it was. The bellman said there were no clocks in casinos, because they didn't want people to know what time it was.

The design of the casino made it impossible to get to a restaurant, a bar, a lounge or even the bathroom without passing the gambling tables.

George Johnson was over at a blackjack table playing two hands at once. He had been thinking about passing up Vegas. The few thousand he'd won the week before at Napa—his rookie season—he lost on the tables in Las Vegas.

There was a true story about one rookie who lost his whole $20,000 bankroll in Las Vegas, called his sponsors and told them he couldn't go any farther, because all their money was gone. They dropped him and he never came back out.

Over on the crap tables in the Sahara, Orville Moody was betting with a big stack of black $100 chips and his caddie Sam was at the same table betting with $5 chips. There was a crowd around to watch Palmer bet.

Tim saw Dave Evans playing craps. Evans was a young player from Texas who didn't even know how to play craps, but was betting anyway—$10 chips, $25 chips. He was losing and still asking the stick-man to explain the game.

Tim watched a rabbit playing craps. The rabbit won three times in a row, then pulled his money off. "Hell," he told the man with him, "the odds are too high against winning that fourth time in a row."

Tim saw Rod Curl at the dice over on the next table, and he wandered over to watch him. Curl was smoking a cigar and drinking 7-Up. Curl watched every bet, knew the odds, and knew where every bet was.

Curl took it easy when he was losing and doubled up when he was winning. He figured that if he was losing, the odds might come back to him sooner or later, but he'd have to have cash to bet with when they did. Tim watched him for a long time, and told him about the rabbit at the next table who'd been afraid to make that fourth bet. "The odds are constant," Curl talked around his cigar. "Against infinity. If you've already won three times in a row, you figure the odds on the fourth one on a one-roll probability." He collected the bets he'd won and stacked them in the rack in front of him. He asked Tim who the player was, and Tim told him. Curl said, "He plays golf the same way. He makes three birdies in a row, then he starts thinking *Uh-uh. Can't make four in a row.* After three birdies, your odds are really better than they were on the first one, because you've just done it right three times in a row."

That next morning, Preevo came to the boys' room with a big box loaded with magazines, shaving cream, razor blades, candy bars, potato chips, corn curls and cigarettes. He gave Tim back the $3 and gave him two packs of cigarettes and some double-edged blades for his trouble. He had got paid that day, and he had come up with what he figured was an ingenious idea—to stock up on all these necessities so that when he lost, he'd be set for the month.

That night there was a pro-am bazaar at the Sahara for people who'd played in the pro-am. There was food and drink and carnival stands with prizes, all compliments of the hotel. Some of the people who played in the Del Webb Pro-Am played free. They were people who had dropped a lot of money at the Sahara over the years, and the free golf was not only a way for the Sahara to show their appreciation but a way to get these people back to the casino where, mathematical probabilities said, they would lose again.

Many of the hookers worked until the sun came up, and were just going home when the first groups were teeing off in the Sahara Invitational that morning.

Curl had another one of those days where he hit the ball the way he wanted, but couldn't get it into the hole. He shot 72, which he didn't consider to be a very good round for a tour pro on that course under the perfect conditions they were playing.

Curl couldn't get it going on Friday either. He had to birdie the last hole to make the cut with his 73. He tried to be philosophical about it. At least he wouldn't have to qualify the next Monday in San Antonio. He had enough to think about without worrying about Mondays. He had made a lot of cuts during the season, and being away from the Monday qualifying had helped his outlook. He thought back to when he had missed his last cut, and it was the first week in July at the Milwaukee Open. And if you made the cuts, there was always a chance that you could get hot the last two days and make a good check.

He didn't get hot that next day. He would get a birdie, then he'd make a bogie. He'd get another birdie, and make another bogie. It sapped the juice out of him, and he came in with a 74, which put him a long way back. All he wanted to do was shoot a solid round and make a check and try again the next week.

He had trouble sleeping that night, so he went to the casino. He saw Chi Chi Rodriguez playing two hands of blackjack at a time. "I can't sleep here," Chi Chi said. "Too much going on." He had missed the cut and had played cards all night the night before.

That night Dave Eichelberger played craps and blackjack until midnight, then headed for his room. He was seven shots off the lead, at 210. Eichelberger, a few years before, had a season in which he made $100,000, finished ninth on the money list, and had won a tournament. The season before this one, however, he'd dropped out of the top sixty. He was currently in sixty-seventh place on the exemption list.

When he got to his room, Eichelberger realized that it was the night of the change from daylight-saving back to mountain standard time. It was really only eleven o'clock. He put on his clothes and hurried back down to the tables. He got hot and he won at blackjack for an hour, doubling up when he'd win. At the end of the hour, he went back up to bed.

His hot streak continued into the next day. He'd shot 70–69–71, but on Sunday he put most of his shots right on the stick and made almost every putt. He shot 64 and sat in the press tent and waited for the finish.

Out on the course that day, the players who weren't in contention were more interested in other scores. It was the football season and they were watching over their bets.

Caddies listened to transistor radios during waits on the tees. As some of the players walked down the fairways, they would yell to other players to try to find out the scores of the games.

All week long, Rod Curl had been trying to make sevens on the crap table, but he made one that Sunday just where he didn't need it—on the golf course, on the sixteenth hole, and he came in with a 74.

John Mahaffey, who had stayed clear of the gambling tables and the night life all week, shot 68–66–69–68 to win the tournament.

Dave Eichelberger's 64 gave him second place all alone and a check for $15,390. He sat down with a pencil in the pressroom and figured his total. It was enough to shoot him into forty-seventh place and cinch the top sixty. He had the switchboard operator in the press tent call long distance to Waco, Texas, and the first words he said to his wife were, "You can plan whatever you want on Mondays next year."

The caddies from Waterloo were packing their bags when there was a knock on the door. It was Preevo. He had bags under his eyes and he stood there with the same box of things he'd brought over a few days before.

Preevo took a slow, deep breath and said, "I was wondering if you fellas would like to buy any magazines, cigarettes, shaving cream, razor blades . . ."

They headed out of town on Highway 93 bound for San Antonio. Tim said that the bellman at the Sahara had been right when he said there were only two kinds of people in Las Vegas—fools and knaves.

Tim felt his light wallet and thought about Preevo. "Yeah," he said, "and they sure don't wait long before they let you know just which one you are."

Rod Curl had won $246.25 in the Sahara Invitational, and as he prepared to fly to San Antonio he was the sixtieth man on the money list with just three tournaments to go.

27

Rollerdromes, Chili Parlors and San Antonio, Texas

Curl knew that he needed a few weeks' rest. It wasn't so much that he was physically tired, even though he had beat balls day after day and had eaten café specials and had woken up to opened suitcases in motel after motel since he'd started grinding in January. But when he played so many weeks in a row with so little rest, he picked up bad habits in his swing, like shifting his weight forward on his toes and shanking, or turning his hands over too fast and duck-hooking. A person could get golfed out, and as he flew toward San Antonio in the last seat in the back of the plane he felt close to it.

San Antonio had never been his favorite tournament. The enthusiasm of Dallas and Fort Worth and Houston in the spring had died in many of the golfers and most of the Texans by the time the San Antonio–Texas Open came around. And the long, hot summers would bake South Texas and leave the fairways so hard that the flat courses all played short, and a player could shoot 68 and still be a long way back in the standings. Any player who knew that and was already pressing would press even more.

When they played the Texas Open at Brackenridge Park Golf Course in San Antonio, before moving it to Woodlake Country Club, it wasn't uncommon to have a lot of 63's and 64's every day. In 1955 at Brackenridge, Mike Souchak, wearing gloves between shots because it was so cold, shot 60, with a 27 on the back nine. You could shoot two under par on occasion and miss the cut.

There was something about the faces in the windows of the bus depots and the downtown drunks and military recruits and chili parlors and rollerdromes that depressed Curl. Maybe because the city was so close to the border, and there were always a lot of sad Mexicans who'd been caught working illegally and were being sent back home.

He wouldn't mind living in a place like Dallas or Fort Worth, but San Antonio was a stop he didn't look forward to—maybe because it was so late in the season.

He stocked up on a lot of sports magazines for the week, and called home every night to talk to his kids. He worked mostly on his putting Monday afternoon and Tuesday, and spent Wednesday around the practice green joking with the caddies.

Rabbit Dyer had a circle around him as he told his stories. Almost all of Rabbit's stories were vaguely connected to some event of major impact. "It was the day Martin Luther King got shot," Rabbit said. "I was sending money home to my kids in a Western Union place, and this girl needed a ride. 'Sure is a lonely town,' I tell her. And late that night, I hear somebody at the door. *Bam, bam, bam. 'Shirley, I know you're in there.'* Ain't but one way out. He shot me and he shot her. Doctor kept sayin', 'You ain't gonna make it, son.' Twelve stitches in the side of my head, Parkland

Memorial Hospital, Dallas, Texas." He took a long pause and pointed. "Exact same room President Kennedy died in."

Tim Schmit's brother was stationed in San Antonio and was getting married that weekend. John Jacobs had gone back to San Diego, but had lined Tim up with a bag for San Antonio, with Jack Ewing.

Some of the caddies were broke after Las Vegas, and some were going downtown trying to sell blood. Some had tried to sell blood in Las Vegas, but there were lines outside most of the places longer than the lines outside a hit movie.

"Man," one caddie said, laying his head back on his golf bag, "I wish I could marry some broad with about five million dollars. She could move me down to Miami, put me under Toski."

Woodlake Country Club wasn't playing so easy this time, but it still wasn't playing tough. Curl putted poorly and shot 73, one over par. The next day, he played a little better and shot 70 and made the cut by two shots.

Mac McLendon missed the cut and could take no more. He had to go home, not just to work on his game, but to rest his nerves and his mind and get off the merry-go-round. He would not go to Pinehurst to try to qualify for the World Open the next week. He would go to Disney World only because his parents lived in Winter Park, just a few miles from Disney World. He was beat down, and he had to go home to decide whether or not he should give it up. He was thirty years old and had a degree in accounting that he'd never used.

He paid Gary St. John his salary and gave him an extra $20. Gary and Tim went to a bachelor party for Tim's brother Irv that night. Irv was stationed in San Antonio and would be getting married the next day. They got drunk and didn't get in till six in the morning. Tim had lost his caddie badge and the guards at the front gate accused him of selling it, and when he got in he was almost late for Ewing's tee time.

Rod Curl shot 71 Saturday and was about two-thirds of the way down the list. He would have to shoot in the 60's the next day to make the kind of check he figured he needed. Whatever he made, it wouldn't be enough for him to clinch the top sixty. He would have to play at the World Open.

Tim Schmit got to see his man's name on the leaderboard for the first time. Jack Ewing had shot 73–70 to make the cut, then shot 68 on Saturday. Sunday he got hot and shot 66, giving him fifth place and $4,812. He gave Tim $130 and told him he'd give him more at the World Open the next week if he'd work for him there.

Curl shot under par, but not enough under par to make any big money. He shot 70 and made $887.23. He left San Antonio the next morning on a flight to North Carolina for the World Open in Pinehurst. There were just two tournaments left, and Curl was in fifty-seventh place, but there was just $750 between him and sixtieth.

28

More Money than the Nobel Prize

The winner of the World Open in Pinehurst would get twice as much money as the winner of the Nobel Peace Prize.

The World Open would be a two-week tournament, eight rounds of golf in an area that was, socially, like being in jail. But it would be for half a million dollars in prize money, more money than the entire 1952 tour was worth, with $100,000 going to the winner and $44,000 going to the runner-up. The tournament was being put on by the Diamondhead Resort Corporation, a builder of homes and condominiums. The Diamondhead Corporation had bought most of Pinehurst, its golf courses and its facilities for $9 million. When they had decided to build a world golf hall of fame, and had put such people as Sandy Koufax and Mickey Mantle on the selection committee, many touring pros criticized the move. Leonard Thompson had said, "That's like building a 747 and asking me to fly it."

Rod Curl wanted a shot at the big prize money in

the World Open so he could make the top sixty. But he was not alone in thinking that this was too much money to put into a tournament. He didn't understand things like tax shelters and write-offs and he knew very little about economics. But he felt a sense of embarrassment playing for this much money when he saw the broken-down rat-colored houses as he made the drive down from the Fayetteville airport.

A few of the other players felt the same way. The president of the corporation had made the comment, half in jest, that here was a tournament that finally had enough money to buy the presence of Jack Nicklaus.

Very soon after, Nicklaus announced that he would not play in the World Open but would go fishing instead.

Tom Weiskopf decided he wouldn't play in it either.

Johnny Miller withdrew.

Lee Trevino said it was too cold and withdrew.

This was the richest tournament in the history of the world. Golfers were coming from all over the world. Press entourages from all over the world. Television all over the world via satellite. The corporation had literally bought itself a major championship. A world championship. *The* world championship. Or so it thought.

After some of the top players withdrew, most of the international press canceled out. And just before the tournament was to begin, the TV network backed out.

It wasn't as if everybody was protesting world hunger. There were other reasons for the lack of interest. The people of the area were great golf fans, but like many of the golfers they were all golfed out. They'd had the Kemper Open in Charlotte, the Greater Greensboro Open, the Match Play and the

L&M Open in Cary, and the Heritage down in Hilton Head, South Carolina. And it was very late in the year —it could get very cold in Pinehurst. The TV network didn't think it could compete with weekend pro football. The tournament committee had arranged for the last day to be on a Saturday, but the network didn't think that the tournament could compete even with college football.

And as far as a world championship was concerned, it was pretty well conceded that whoever was the top player in America was the top player in the world. Hardly anyone took seriously the challenges of Oscar Cerda, Francisco Abreu, Fidel Deluca, or Mohammed Säid Moussa, if they indeed knew or cared who they were. The people of North Carolina did not have the slightest idea how to say "charge" in Chinese, and a name like Toni Kugelmüeller probably wouldn't even fit on the leaderboard.

Of the quality European players, Tony Jacklin had stayed in Europe, and about the only foreign player who was going to add to the gate, a fellow named Gary Player, was down in Florida and could got there on an overnight Greyhound.

The tournament would be played on Thursday, Friday, Saturday and Sunday of the first week, then on Wednesday, Thursday and Friday, and finally conclude on Saturday of the second week.

On Monday of the first week of the tournament the hotels and motels in and around Pinehurst already had more vacant rooms than they cared to think about. Most of the hotels had turned down reservations to house the foreign press, the network people and the many foreign fans who also wouldn't show.

Two reporters checked into the Holly Inn near the old town square. "Where's the action?" one of them asked.

A bellman scratched his head. "Action?" He

thought on it. "Oh. Well, we got a bar here in the hotel. Open till ten-thirty too."

"God," the reporter said. "What do the swingers do?"

The bellman smiled. "Oh, heck, they go on over to the Pinehurst Hotel. That place stays open till midnight."

Besides the other troubles that had befallen the tournament, the greens had been overseeded during the transition from Bermuda to bent grass. The greens were hard and bumpy. And there had been a drought since the middle of September.

Gibby Gilbert, a man who has been known to gamble and a touring pro from Florida, came in that first day with one of the greatest rounds ever played. Pinehurst's Number Two course had a reputation as one of the toughest in the world. And besides there being bumpy greens, it was unseasonably cold on Thursday.

Just the year before, Gilbert had felt about the tour what Mac McLendon now felt. He was ready to quit and take a job as a traveling rep with a golf equipment company. But Jack Nicklaus talked him into going to Jack Grout, who had been Nicklaus's lifelong instructor. Grout had showed Gilbert how to fade his shots properly, and so far in the season, Gilbert had won $53,000.

He shot a 32–30 for a 62 on Pinehurst Number Two that first day, and he was five shots closer to that $100,000 than the nearest man.

Rod Curl opened up with a dismal 78. He kept reminding himself that he could still do well, since the tournament was eight rounds instead of four, and he wanted to make sure he made the cut so he'd at least be in at Disney World.

It stayed cold and so did Curl. He duplicated his feat of the day before—another 78. But the cut wouldn't be made until after the fourth round, and he tried to keep himself psyched up. The greens were frozen when the morning groups teed off on Saturday. There was ice in the bunkers, and the players wore heavy sweaters and gloves and stocking caps. Very few people showed up to watch.

Curl had his best day in that cold weather. He shot 70 and had a good chance, if he shot another good round, of surviving the cut and maybe making a good check.

But he couldn't handle it on Sunday. He came in with a 79. He would get a $500 guarantee, but he would have to qualify at Disney unless he could get a sponsor exemption. Puzzled, disgusted and worn out, he packed his bags and flew back to Redding.

The foreign flags still flew around the Pinehurst clubhouse, but only four foreign players had made the cut. Mohammed Säid Moussa had headed back for the sand bunkers of Egypt, Hsieh Min Nan had gone back to Taiwan, and Seung Hack Kim, having lived up to his middle name, caught the first thing going to Korea.

Some of the golf promoters had come to Pinehurst in hopes of finding out everything they could about the world golf market. Golf had been growing, especially in Japan. Jumbo Ozaki, the hero of Japanese golf, was making about a million dollars a year in side money over there. Department-store lines of clubs sold for $600 and more. Since there was so little land and so much demand, the Japanese were building driving ranges that took memberships and required starting times. There was even some new pop religion over there based on, of all things, the game of golf.

Japanese who had no idea who the President of the United States was knew who Arnie and Jack were.

Lu Liang-huan of Taiwan had made the cut and won over many American players and what little gal-

lery there had been. Alfonso Bohorques of Colombia
and Dale Hayes of South Africa had also made the
cut, but they were all a long way out of contention.

The fourth foreigner to make the cut was Gary
Player. Player was a mysterious man in many little
ways. He was very mystical, a health fanatic who was
big on the power of positive thinking. He was also
very religious, a sort of fundamentalist who would
write down quotations from the Bible and carry them
with him. One of his biggest heroes was Billy Graham. Many people doubted Player's sincerity. When
he first joined the American tour, he was a very vocal
defender of South Africa's apartheid policies. He
rarely said anything about those policies anymore,
although he didn't come out and criticize them. His
gimmick, if it could be called that, was diplomacy. In
all of his speeches, he would talk about what a great
country whatever country he happened to be in was.
Were he to land in hell, his critics said, he would
probably immediately start talking about what a
wonderful place it was.

Those who doubted Player's sincerity off the golf
course had no doubts about his abilities on it. He had
shot 68 on Saturday, the day of the ice. But he was still
thirteen shots back of Gibby Gilbert, who had shot 280
for the first four rounds and was trying to go wire-to-
wire.

Gary St. John and Mike Brogan caught a bus to
Charlotte and got a Delta flight bound ultimately for
Waterloo, Iowa. Their men had missed the cut and
they were running low on money. They decided
they'd had enough and it was time to go back home.

Roger Mastain's man had missed the cut too, and
he had just enough money to buy a bus ticket to
Waterloo. He headed back to the nine-to-five world
and time clocks and monthly bills—and monthly salaries.

Tim Schmit and Bob Starbuck stayed for the last week of the tournament because their men had made the cut. Starbuck was caddying for Rick Rhoads, who was up there in the running at 290.

Some of the black caddies had girl friends in the general area. The young white caddies had located a girl named Becky who, although she wasn't beautiful, was cute enough, and more important, dependable— and as it turned out, about the only game in town.

When the second half of the tournament began on Wednesday, the weather had changed completely. The temperatures went into the sixties and so did Tom Watson. When Gilbert shot his 62, the experts of golf had said that a round like that wouldn't likely be duplicated on Pinehurst Number Two for another fifty years. But Watson went into a trance on Wednesday and made three birdies on the front side, then birdied six holes and eagled another on the back side, for a 62.

Gilbert had finally lost the lead, with three rounds to play. And although Watson shot 76 the next day, he held on to the lead. On Friday he shot another 76 and still had the lead. Gilbert had finally felt the pressure and had shot 82.

Miller Barber was in second place that last day, two shots back of Watson. Barber was far from a business manager's dream. He was portly and bald, forty-two years old, with a swing that looked like a hacker's. He wore tinted glasses that looked like sunglasses and hid his eyes, but he was called Mr. X for another reason—because of his swing. Nobody seemed to know why or how his swing worked. He swung flat, flew his right elbow and looped like a 21-handicapper. But somehow his shots went straight. He was a good putter and one of the straightest drivers in the world when the heat was on.

And the heat was on.

Watson lost the lead early, and Barber, Ben Crenshaw and Leonard Thompson battled for it.

But it was Miller Barber who won the $100,000. When he made his last putt, he jumped up in the air, and jumped on the money list all the way from thirty-second to sixth.

On the victory stand near the eighteenth green one of the heads of the resort corporation gave a long-winded speech and mistakenly introduced Leonard Thompson, the third-place finisher as Tom Watson. Thompson had been raised just a few miles from there, and several people from his hometown had come up to cheer him on. "That's about like these people," one of his hometowners said. "They don't give him an invitation, don't ask him to play in their pro-am, and when he almost wins their tournament, they forget his name."

A woman who'd been at the back of the crowd called to her husband. "Barber Miller won it."

Her husband scratched his head and said, "Who the hell is Barbara Miller?"

When Miller Barber got his check, his only speech was a loud "WOO-PIG-SOOEY."

The golfers would go home to rest. There would be a one-week break between the World Open and the Walt Disney World Golf Classic, the last tournament of the season.

Allen Miller and Bob Goalby moved into the top sixty with World Open money.

And Rod Curl dropped out.

There was one tournament left to play.

29

Checking the Mail

Curl had practiced at home while the last week of the World Open was being played. He wasn't exempt for the Walt Disney World Golf Classic, so he called, and explaining his situation, asked for a sponsor exemption. The person on the tournament committee he had talked to told him that they would give him an exemption. But he was taking no chances. He had learned a hard lesson at Tucson when a technicality had kept him out of the tournament. He knew that a phone call didn't make it official. He was sure that the other players who were close to the top sixty and weren't exempt for the Disney had also called asking for sponsor exemptions. For things to be official, there had to be a letter.

Curl practiced his game all that week before the Disney while he waited for a letter from the tournament committee. He had a good week of practice, and by the end of the week there was still no letter.

He headed for Disney World prepared to qualify on Monday.

30

The End of a Season

In the entrance to Cinderella's Castle in the Magic Kingdom of Walt Disney World, harps echo and a sweet voice sings, "A dream . . . is a wish . . . your heart makes—" And if you didn't see the ceiling speakers or the souvenir shop at the exit, you might believe that Cinderella was really up there, doing whatever it is that Cinderella does.

It's part of the commerce at Disney World—a subtle, creative commerce. Several companies, from Greyhound to Welch's grape juice, have paid millions of dollars just to be the official whatever of Disney World. Walter Elias Disney didn't live to see the opening of his Florida spectacle, but he knew how to make fun a multimillion-dollar business, and how to make a multimillion-dollar business fun. The players had brought their families—to relax, ride the horse-drawn streetcars, eat ice cream and bring the season to a happy end.

It would take all of that, plus somewhere around $3,000 to make it a happy ending for Rod Curl. Allen

Miller and Bob Goalby had moved into the top sixty, and Curl, Andy North and Dwight Nevil, having missed the World Open cut, had dropped out of it.

And the PGA point standings told them exactly where they stood with reality:

58.	Bob Goalby	47,538.93
59.	Chuck Courtney	46,908.79
60.	Allen Miller	46,431.93
61.	Dwight Nevil	46,127.85
62.	Rod Curl	45,368.89
63.	Andy North	44,889.90

Curl was exactly $1,063.04 behind Allen Miller, but he had made up his mind that if he was to go down, he would go down shooting.

And when he got to the tournament, he found out that he would not have to qualify. The tournament committee had granted him a sponsor exemption. But they had granted exemptions to Nevil and North also.

Curl checked into a room at the Polynesian Village Hotel on Disney property, where most of the pros stayed. The rooms were 50 percent off to the pros.

Tim Schmit hadn't had a room the first night he was at Disney World. He had loaned Bob Starbuck enough money to take the limousine and head back to Waterloo, and with just $9 and a heavy backpack, he hitched down to Orlando for the tournament. His troubles started early. When he finally got a ride, it was with two freaks who fornicated in the back seat in broad daylight while Tim was taking his turn at the wheel. He spent his first night dozing and drinking coffee in the booth of an all-night café. He caddied practice rounds and shagged for pocket money at the Lake Buena Vista course, where the qualifying would be held. He spent Thanksgiving there, eating the free sandwiches the Disney people had given the caddies.

Tim got a room at the Days Inn until his money ran out and he had to leave. Jack Ewing had promised him extra money after his finish at San Antonio, and he had won over $2,000 at Pinehurst and still didn't give him the bonus he'd promised. He said he'd take care of him at Disney World.

By Tuesday Tim was down to $4.87, and he went to Disney World that night to see whether he could run into some caddies and find a place to sleep. A security guard spotted him walking through the restaurant with a backpack on and made him leave the property. There was no place he was allowed to camp, except at Fort Wilderness for $12.

Tim eased down onto the golf course and climbed the TV tower at the fifteenth hole, rolled his sleeping bag out, and spent the night there.

Curl spent Monday night looking out at the Seven Seas lagoon and the Castle of Cinderella, which rose up a hundred and eighty feet out of the theme park and lit the place up like the Taj Mahal.

Tim Schmit waited for daylight and some activity around the clubhouse before he came down off the tower. He was hungry and needed a shower and a good shampoo. When he went to pick up his caddie uniform, he found out that Jack Ewing had withdrawn from the tournament. That very morning, Ewing had told Tim that he was coming, and Tim had passed up two jobs. He wanted to hitch home, but he was too broke even to hitchhike.

Rod Curl had breakfast in his room Wednesday morning. The tournament would begin that day, because Hughes Television Network didn't want to compete with Sunday pro football. They would televise only the last round, and it would end on Saturday, December first.

On a piece of hotel stationery, Curl jotted down the money breakdown for a $150,000 tournament:

1st:	20%	$30,000
2nd:	11.4%	17,100
3rd:	7.1%	10,650
4th:	4.7%	7,050
5th:	4.1%	6,150
6th:	3.6%	5,400
7th:	3.2%	4,800
8th:	2.9%	4,425
9th:	2.7%	4,050
10th:	2.5%	3,750

He figured that there was a chance he could make about $2,000 and still get into the top sixty, but he couldn't be sure. Unless something freaky happened and everybody below him made big checks, he knew that $3,000 would put him into the top sixty for sure, because there were players who were exempt for other reasons, tournament winners and the like, who were holding down spots in fifty-fifth, fifty-sixth and fifty-seventh places and weren't entered in the Disney. If he could make $3,000 he could move into their spots.

Tim Schmit sold some golf balls to get meal money. He ran into a magazine writer he'd come to know on the tour and told him about his predicament. The writer had an extra bed in his room, which was at the Golf Resort Hotel, right there on the property. He told Tim that if he'd do some gofer work for him, he would give Tim a place to stay and a few meals.

The Golf Resort Hotel was where most of the press was being housed. Disney World used two courses for its golf classic, and both courses bordered the hotel. The first two days, the players would alternate between the tight, watery Palm course, and the long, more wide open Magnolia course. The last two days would be on the Magnolia, where Curl figured he'd have an advantage over players who couldn't hit it as far as he could, because if the wind blew hard—and he hoped it would—he could still reach the par-fives in two.

His game was ready.

All he wanted to do was shoot 70 or 71 that first day on the Palm and be in position to attack Magnolia.

Curl teed off at 12:40 on Wednesday and he was nervous.

He birdied the first hole, and it loosened him up some.

Curl shot 35 on the front side, avoided all the lakes and ponds and birdied 17 and 18 for a 69. He was a happy man as he headed for the press tent to check the other scores. But he knew he had a long way to go.

The players in the running for the top sixty—anybody with any vague chance—were in the press tent checking each other's scores when they finished their rounds.

The scores were in alphabetical order:

Courtney, Chuck LaJolla, Calif.	77
Curl, Rod Redding, Calif.	69
Goalby, Bob Amana, Iowa	74

He read farther down the list:

Miller, Allen Pensacola, Fla.	75
Nevil, Dwight Kilgore, Texas	69
North, Andy Gainesville, Fla.	75

Curl had to make $758.97 more than Nevil, who was one slot ahead of him, and $1,063.05 more than Allen Miller, in sixtieth.

The writer Tim was doing gofer work for was on expenses, and he knew all sorts of ways to get things for free—hotel rooms, rental cars, meals, drinks, clothes, shoes, golf balls. The Disney publicity department had paid the plane fares of several members of the press and were putting them up at the hotel to publicize it and to enhance the Disney World golf image.

Tim decided to shave his beard because he was afraid the security guards would recognize him and start grilling him, maybe even get him tossed out of the hotel. When Tim walked down to the lobby with the press badge on, the security guard who'd run him off opened the door and did a little bow.

They ate in the restaurant at the hotel that night and ordered steak and rock lobster combos. The writer laughed and said, "The meek inherit nothing."

Tim thought about the people he'd got a ride with to Orlando and he said, "I think they inherit each other."

Rod Curl was well aware of what the meek inherit. He was tied for eighth place with ten players, with three rounds to play. He had supper that night with Bob Graham and Graham's wife and some friends of theirs. He had met Graham on the tour when he was a rookie and Graham was tending bar at a country club. That night he watched TV and worked on his putting alignment.

A cold norther kept the natives inside their homes on Thursday, and it blew papers across the first tee of the Magnolia. Curl's group went off at 9:55.

He was sailing along with pars, and then the wheels started coming off. He was choking. He had to scramble just to sink two long putts for bogies. He made the turn in 39, and he told his caddie on the tenth tee, "We're even-par for the tournament. Hell, we make a couple bogies and we might miss the cut." He looked up, and with as much humor as he could manage, he said, "Don't get off me now."

The tenth was a 526-yard par-five. He hit a drive almost three hundred yards, but it rolled into the deep rough. He hit a four-iron just short, then stuck a wedge shot six feet and rolled the putt in for a birdie.

He was back to −1 for the tournament.

He parred the eleventh and bogied the twelfth and went back to even-par. He made a six-footer on thirteen to save par.

Then he hit two big wood shots within thirty yards of the 592-yard fourteenth, and birdied it to go back to −1.

The fifteenth was a long par-three. "Hey, this is a car hole," he told his caddie. His three-iron headed right at the stick, and as the ball hit the cup, Curl yelled out, *"Ten thousand dollars."* It bounced out and rolled fifteen feet past. But he rolled the putt in and went back to −2.

He put his second shot ten feet from the cup on sixteen . . . and rolled it in.

The seventeenth was a long par-four dog-legging around a lake. If you cut the lake the long way, you could have a short-iron left to the green; if you played too cozy, you could have a wood or maybe couldn't get home. But if you tried to cut it too short, you might end up in the lake. Curl figured it was a good time to gamble, and he went at the farthest conceivable point. A marshal said to another, "Kid must carry his balls in a wheelbarrow."

Curl put it eight feet with a nine-iron and rolled it in.

On eighteen he put his second shot ten feet from

the cup and dropped it for a birdie.

And a 32 on the back side.

He'd made five birdies in a row, and instead of missing the cut, he was in with a 71, and he headed for the press tent to check the scores:

Courtney, Chuck LaJolla, Calif.	77 72	149
Curl, Rod Redding, Calif.	69 71	140
Goalby, Bob Amana, Iowa	74 74	148
Miller, Allen Pensacola, Fla.	75 72	147

He had to wait to see what Nevil and North had shot, because they weren't in yet. Curl sat in the press tent and drank Pepsi's and waited. Finally the woman wrote down the scores:

Nevil, Dwight Kilgore, Texas	69 70	139
North, Andy Gainesville, Fla.	74 76	150

They all had to wait to see what the cut would be. It was finally made: 147 was in, 148 was down the road. North, Goalby and Courtney were out of the tournament. Courtney was $1,539.90 ahead of Curl. Goalby was $2,170.04 ahead of Curl. But he was still behind Miller and Nevil, so he had to beat them both. And there was always the chance of somebody a few notches down making a big check and bumping him out. He figured the best way to do it was not to think about other players but to try to make the $3,000 that he knew would cinch the top sixty.

In the press tent, Nevil told the reporters, "I'm here for one reason and one reason only. And that's to make the top sixty."

A reporter said, "You're only two shots out of the lead. What if you get into position to win?"

"If I get into position to win," Nevil said, "I might make a charge at it, but that's not likely."

They asked Curl the same things when they questioned him. "I think you can *make* yourself do things," he said. "I wouldn't mind if the greens were just a hair faster. But three shots off the lead, I'm not about to gripe."

"What if you get into position to win," the same reporter asked. "Would you make a charge at it?"

Curl pulled the microphone in close. "I sure would."

And he went out to the practice tee to hit wedge shots.

Tim Schmit could use his press pass to get into the Magic Kingdom theme park. He and the writer rode the monorail over, and they wandered up and down the 1890's Main Street, shook hands with Donald Duck and saw a silent movie. They went through all the attractions in Tomorrowland, saw the Hall of Presidents and rode the Mississippi stern-wheeler *Admiral Joe Fowler.* At 5:30, the whole Disney World band marched through Cinderella's Castle playing parade music and all the characters of Disney World danced along behind.

There was this great absence of tension inside the park. No sad, beaten-down faces, no bill collectors, no anxiety, no pushing and shoving and cussing each other. It was a world of its own, a fantasy world something like the golf tour if a person looked at it from the outside.

They ate big meals, closed down the lounge show in the Polynesian that night, and with the aid of two girls who worked at Disney they commandeered a golf cart and rode around the property drinking wine until almost five in the morning.

Rod Curl had been in bed early, and he slept well.

It was warm and there was a light wind Friday morning when the threesome of Rod Curl, Grier Jones and Jack Nicklaus was announced on the first tee at 10:42.

Curl could see the leaderboard as he stood on the tee:

Name	*Hole*	*Score*
MAHAFFEY	36	−7
NEVIL	36	−5
MORGAN	36	−5
STARKS	36	−5
L. GRAHAM	36	−5
NELSON	36	−5
D. GRAHAM	36	−4
BROWN	36	−4
CURL	36	−4
PAYNE	36	−4
JONES	36	−4
NICKLAUS	36	−3

While they waited for the group ahead of them to hit their second shots, Curl's caddie said, "You know, I'll bet if a man just hit the ball right where Jack hit it every time, he couldn't go too wrong."

Curl said, "Hell, I wanna drive it *past* him, putt it better than him, and I want to beat him." He took his head-cover off his driver and handed it to his caddie. "I'd like to *drown* him today."

They had a gallery three times the size of the leader's gallery, just to see Jack. Playing with someone like Nicklaus inspired Curl, but better yet, it made him keep his mind on his game.

They both parred the first two holes. On the third hole, Curl made a thirty-footer, and as the putt rolled into the cup, his caddie threw a right cross and yelled *"Pow."*

They moved Curl's name up on the leaderboard and put a −5 next to it.

He was outdriving Nicklaus on every hole. On the ninth, he hit it forty yards past Nicklaus, hit a cut-five-iron fifteen feet and dropped the putt for a birdie. He outdrove Nicklaus again on the tenth, and Nicklaus laughed and shrugged to the gallery. "I don't have an answer for it either."

Curl birdied ten, made two bogies and one birdie, and by the time they came to seventeen, Curl was −7 for the tournament, tied with Nicklaus for the round and one shot ahead of him for the tournament. But Jack could go all out and Curl now had to protect his score. Nicklaus went for it on his drive and cleared the lake at the farthest point. Curl played safe, hit a fade out to the right and had a five-iron left to the green. Nicklaus had a nine-iron. Curl put it in the trap and bogied, Nicklaus hit it four feet and birdied.

When Curl birdied the eighteenth for a 69, the gallery gave him a long ovation.

He went to the press tent to check the scores:

Curl, Rod Redding, Calif.	69 71 69	209
Miller, Allen Pensacola, Fla.	75 72 73	220

Nevil was just finishing. He'd missed a lot of chances with short chips and putts. He missed his putt on eighteen and shot 74, and the scorekeeper put it up on the board in the press tent:

Nevil, Dwight   69 70 74   213
Kilgore, Texas

Curl told the reporters, "How can you choke when you're playing with the best player in the world. I wish I could play with him again tomorrow."

Everything was a fight now. He had four shots on Nevil, but Nevil could turn things around the next day, and Curl still had to make $1,063.04 more than Allen Miller, or enough to pass Courtney and Goalby —and Mason Rudolph, who had started the tournament in seventy-second place on the exemption list was now tied for second place in the tournament. He could make a big check and move up too.

As Curl left the course that evening he looked up at the leaderboard and studied it:

Name	*Hole*	*Score*
MAHAFFEY	54	−10
RUDOLPH	54	− 8
NICKLAUS	54	− 8
STARKS	54	− 8
MORGAN	54	− 8
SCHLEE	54	− 8
GREEN	54	− 7
M. BARBER	54	− 7
CURL	54	− 7
BLANCAS	54	− 6
D. GRAHAM	54	− 6

He had a lot on his mind that night. He went to bed at 10:30 but he didn't get to sleep until way past midnight. He had played in forty-three tournaments during the season, and now it all came down to eighteen holes.

Curl teed off at 11:50 that last day in the third-to-last group. He was playing with Hubert Green and

Pete Brown, a good pairing for him because he liked them both and usually played well when he played with Hubert. It was a beautiful day, the temperature somewhere in the 70's. Curl knew that on that course under those conditions, he'd have to shoot 70 or 71 to hold his position in the tournament. A 72 might lose ground. He had to hold his position and hope that nothing crazy happened.

He drove down the middle on the first hole. He parred the first hole, parred the second, and made an eight-footer for a par on the third.

Mason Rudolph birdied the first hole and moved into second all alone.

Curl was counting on a birdie on the fifth hole, a par-five. He was on the fringe in two and had a short chip, his specialty, but he flinched and knocked it ten feet by and missed coming back. "That's a gift I gave everybody," he mumbled.

He drove into the rough on the next hole and was 160 from the pin with the wind behind him. He hit an eight-iron, but it was one of those downwind fliers that went 180 yards and over the green into the high grass. He made a double-bogie and went three-over for the day. He would have to par in just to shoot 75. He was hurting and he knew it.

"Typical damn finish of mine," he said to his caddie. "I'm throwing it all out the back door on one round." Mason Rudolph was still in second place, and he didn't know what Nevil was doing.

The sixth hole was a par-three. "I got one-ninety-four to the pin," his caddie said.

"How deep's the green behind the pin?" Curl said.

"Sixteen yards."

"You sure?"

"I walked it."

"What do you think?" Curl said.

"I think four-iron. What do you think?"

"I think four-iron too."

He put the best swing he could on the four-iron, it drew in and bit twenty feet from the pin.

His putt would break left, slightly downhill. He stroked it, gave it a lot of body English as it headed for the cup, his caddie rooted it home and it droppèd in the side door for a birdie.

He hit an eight-iron out of the rough on the seventh hole eight feet from the pin and rolled another birdie in. He was back to where he could par in for a 73, but he knew that might not be good enough.

On the next hole, Pete Brown hit into the woods and they had to get a ruling. It took twenty minutes and they had to let Nicklaus's group play through. Curl was tight and missed the green on the par-five, then missed his birdie putt.

He rimmed a birdie on nine.

He was counting on a birdie on the tenth, but he hit one into the trap, flinched coming out and missed the putt. He was still one over par for the day.

He rimmed a birdie on eleven and hit one in the deep rough on his second shot to twelve. He had to try a cut shot. It wasn't his shot, but he had to try it. There was very little room between the edge of the green and the pin, and he needed a par. He opened the blade of his sand wedge, swept under it, and the ball went straight up and came down softly just over the bunker, bounced and stopped six feet away. He made the putt and got his par.

He almost drove the thirteenth with the longest drive of the day, but he flinched again on the chip shot and couldn't make the eight-footer coming back.

The fourteenth was a 592-yard par-five.

He hit a drive that carried 280, and when they got to the ball, the caddie said they had 292 yards left to the pin. Curl hit a three-wood with everything he had, and as the ball took off he knew he'd got it good. "Go,

you bitch," his caddie yelled. The ball hit just short,
but it took a big hop and rolled onto the edge. He was
sixty feet from the pin.

It was a speed putt, downhill with a left-to-right
break of about six inches right at the hole. He wanted
to putt it close and make his birdie. The ball started
out left, broke right and slowed down, slid, then
dropped right into the center of the cup for an eagle.

He had brought it back. He was −8 for the tournament. All he had to do was hang onto the club. He
played gimme all the way in, and as he made his last
five-foot putt of the season on eighteen, Bob Toski and
Ray Scott were announcing in the TV tower. The
camera gave a close-up shot, and inside the press tent
the people watching could see Curl make the putt and
hear Toski say, ". . . which will, incidentally, put Rod
Curl into the top sixty."

The Walt Disney World band was already march-
ing down the eighteenth fairway, and all the Disney
characters in their costumes did a victory dance on
the green for the winner, Jack Nicklaus, and for the
people who'd stayed for the presentations.

But inside the tent, it wasn't quite over.

Tom Place sat down in the tent with a pencil while
Dwight Nevil and Rod Curl and Allen Miller looked
over his shoulder. Mason Rudolph had finished second and his $17,100 moved him from seventy-second
all the way to fiftieth, moving Allen Miller out. Kenny
Still called on the phone for his friend Chuck Courtney to see how it came out. Courtney had dropped out
of it too.

Curl had finished ninth in the tournament all
alone and had won $4,050 and moved into the top
sixty. He had made it.

Dwight Nevil had shot 72, which put him at 285
for the tournament. It would give him, they finally
figured, $1,065.

That was not enough. Nevil stared at the sheet. He sat down and figured it again, but it came out the same:

58.	Rod Curl	49,793.89
59.	Gary Player	47,582.14
60.	Bob Goalby	47,538.93
61.	Dwight Nevil	47,192.85

Nevil was numb. He realized that all he would've had to do was shoot one stroke better and he would've made $510 more, and passed Bob Goalby for sixtieth place.

As he left the tent he glanced quickly at Curl, who was drinking a cold Pepsi and telling the press he was going to celebrate with something better than Pepsi. "But tomorrow I'm flying home," he said. "I'm gonna work on my bunker play and my driver. If I can learn to play out of the bunkers better and drive it straight, I can make that hundred thousand next year. That's my goal. A hundred thousand next year."

The caddies said good-byes, paid debts, bets, and stalled for time. The players packed their cars and headed for home.

And while Dwight Nevil sat alone in the locker room, Bob Graham had already got a table in the clubhouse and they were icing down champagne for Rod Curl.

The next morning Tim Schmit got a money order from a friend at home. He'd started out with big ideas —get lucky and get the winner, come home in a top hat. He was on foot now, he'd been stiffed and had ended up in the hole. He'd seriously considered staying at Disney World to work, but he got to thinking that the lobby of the Contemporary Hotel might not look so exotic if you had to come in the employees' entrance through the kitchen every day.

It was the same way with the pro golf tour. He would keep Disney World and the tour as nice places to visit sometime. There were a lot of other things he could do, and he wanted to go home to find out just what and how well.

Before he left that Sunday morning, the magazine writer gave him four small wallet cards that read:

I AM A DEAF MUTE
HELP SUPPORT MY FAMILY
GOD BLESS YOU

He caught a ride with a trucker at the junction of I-4 and Highway 27, heading all the way to St. Louis.

Curl slept in Sunday morning. He woke into a new world. He took his time packing and had breakfast served in his room. He had made—with his pro-am money and prize-money from satellites—over $50,000 for the season. But best of all, there would be no more Mondays.

The real significance of what Curl had accomplished wasn't in the fact that he made a lot of money playing golf. The significance was that he was somebody who had set out to attain something, had overcome adversity, and had made it. Not so spectacular as Lindbergh crossing the Atlantic, but significant just the same.

He rode to the airport that day with a friend he'd met during the season. They talked about his finish.

"What kind of cigar is that you're smoking?" the friend asked.

"Hell, I don't know," Curl said. "It cost sixty cents. That's about all I know."

He put his feet up on the seatback and they talked about $100,000 players, about testimonials and commercials and exhibitions, and about what would happen if he ever started winning.

Curl stopped talking and told the driver to hit the brakes. There was a hitchhiker on the side of the highway with a suitcase. The driver backed up and Curl rolled down the window. "We're headed for the airport. We could give you a lift that far."

The hitchhiker said he was going the other way, up the turnpike.

"Goin' home, I bet," Curl said.

"Yeah, Louisville. I want to get there tomorrow."

"That's a long haul."

The hitchhiker shrugged. "Yeah, well, I'll make it."

Curl looked at the hitchhiker, and he reached down into his pocket, pulled out some wadded bills, got a ten and a twenty, put the money in the hitchhiker's hand and said, "Here. Take the bus."

Back at the golf course, the name tags of the touring pros have been taken off the lockers. The tee markers have been moved back up front for weekend guests in motorized carts.

But it's quiet now. The TV towers are down. The names are off the leaderboard and scraps of paper blow across the fairways.

Out on the seventeenth green, a marshal's sign is stuck in the fringe of the green.

The sign says:

Q
U
I
E
T

It's December.

The birds have come, the tents are down, the circus is gone and the season is over.

About the Author

DAN GLEASON received his degree in journalism from the University of Iowa and began writing about golf by doing humor pieces and fiction for *Golf Magazine*. To research all the aspects of the pro golf tour, he drove courtesy cars, set up playing exhibitions for pros, caddied, bus-boyed, worked for a network golf show, and sold souvenirs at a tournament. He has been a contributing editor for a golf magazine and has regularly published both fiction and nonfiction in national magazines.